THE CITY
WHERE
NO ONE DIES

THE CITY
WHERE
NO ONE DIES

Bernard Dadié

Translated by Janis Mayes

Three Continents Press

Contents

BERNARD DADIÉ: POLITICS, LITERATURE AND THE AESTHETICS OF THE *CHRONIQUE*

For more than a half century, Bernard Binlin Dadié has been distinguished as the leading and most prolific writer from the Ivory Coast. His reputation extends beyond these national boundaries. The powerful discourse of African consciousness embodied in his literature, fused with the artist's particular handling of narrative, poetic and dramatic forms, accounts for Dadié's sustained recognition as one of Africa's leading writers.

Because Dadié writes in French, the *lingua franca* of the Ivory Coast, his works have not been easily accessible to anglophone audiences. Like most African writers of his generation, Dadié uses a European language, the by-product of European hegemony. Along with the artificial boundaries drawn by colonial powers in Africa came foreign languages used deliberately as tools of empowerment and artifacts of culture. In the specific example of the Ivory Coast, sixty African languages comprise a significant part of the country's linguistic matrix. Therefore, one of the primary roles of the critic of African literatures in European languages is to analyze and assess a writer's handling of language in illuminating particular African experiences, milieux and ambience. To date, English translations exist for relatively few of Dadié's works, which may account for the limited critical studies on his literature in the anglophone world.

Born an N'Zima in Assinie, Ivory Coast, in 1914, Dadié was decisively shaped by the community, where traditional values were taught and upheld.[1] Especially instrumental in Dadié's classic African formation during those early and impressionable years were two members of his family, his father, Gabriel Binlin Dadié, and his uncle, Melantchi. The father, an influential and highly respected member of the community, was a successful planter and one of the founders of the "Syndicat des Planteurs Africains," a union of African planters in the Ivory Coast.[2] He was also a powerful member of the

1

Partie Démocratique de la Côte d'Ivoire (Democratic Party of the Ivory Coast).[3]

At an early age Dadié went to live with his uncle Melantchi, a farmer in Bingerville, near Abidjan, the capital of the Ivory Coast. One of the most important things that Dadié learned during these years was the need and the ability to live responsibly and cooperatively as a member of a family and a community. While learning to live in this manner, the young Dadié came to accept this philosophy of life as fundamental.[4] Undoubtedly, it was during these early years that Dadié began to develop his deep spirituality and an understanding of African philosophies and cultures. Even today, Dadié does not reduce the world to the level of an inert object functioning according to physical laws alone. Rather, he believes that a person is an integral part of the universe. Such a concept is based on more than an intellectual system that places emphasis on observation and logical deduction to the exclusion of other cognitive processes. Myths, legends, rituals, ceremonies and various other elements, all of which are integral parts of community life, are used to explain the world. Dadié is a writer whose inspirations are drawn from these sources of African culture and society.

Since the Ivory Coast was established as an official colony of France in 1893 and did not receive its constitutional independence until 1960, Dadié experienced firsthand repressive French colonial domination in both its practical and theoretical dimensions. This part of his life is manifest in myriad aspects of the writer's work, often reified in his depiction of the painful ironies inherent in the formal French education he received. Dadié received his primary and secondary schooling in the Ivory Coast at the "Ecole du Quartier de France" in Grand Bassam and at the "Ecole Supérieure" in Bingerville. While his childhood and adolescence were spent in the land of his birth, the young writer lived in Dakar, Senegal from 1935 to 1947. There he studied at the "Ecole William Ponty" and was awarded the degree, "Diplôme de Commis d'Administration" with a specialization in administration. As an active member of the theatre group at William Ponty, Dadié wrote several plays, the most famous of which, *Assémien Déhylé* (1936), is contextualized in a viable pre-colonial Agni village in the Ivory Coast. After Ponty, Dadié worked as a journalist for *Le Réveil*, the newspaper of the *Rassemblement Démocratique Africain* (RDA). These were embattled times, which, when reconstructed, correspond to the height of organized Pan-African resistance to French colonial rule and nascent African nationalism.

It is during this period that Dadié began to carve out his place in African literary traditions. His poetry and political essays of this period evoke in various ways the colonial experience and affirm his African heritage. As a young writer Dadié adopted an ideology to which he still adheres regarding the role and nature of African literature and the responsibility of the artist to the community. This is how Dadié expresses it:

> Our people...is a people who has, more than any other right, the right to
> an intelligible literature....Literature...is a resource, a weapon, I mean to
> say that it is foremost, an alarm or war drum....Suppose that our writers
> speak and no one understands them, sing and no one hears them,
> wouldn't this be a breakup of the community, a reinforcement of slavery,
> an increment of our death—in life?[5]

Embodied in Dadié's ideology of literature is the concept of a well defined
political position that is determined in great measure by a special relationship to an intended audience, and a decipherable pretext for writing. In
many respects these notions are paradigmatic to that of a griot in some traditional African societies. Dadié's social, educational and political development, the knowledge of the community of which he is a part and the strong
responsibility he feels toward it, have remarkably influenced his literature.

That Dadié should adopt such a stance is especially significant in light
of a French colonial policy of assimilation which argued, in part, that African
culture was inherently inferior to the culture of the French. As an active
member of the *Rassemblement Démocratique Africain* in Senegal until
1947, Dadié was involved in an organized struggle to dismantle French
colonialism and imperialism in West Africa. His literature of the period,
consisting largely of poetry and essays, serves as a battleground designed
to express and illuminate a particular vision of life in Africa. At a time when
the Negritude Movement was in full swing in Paris with writers such as
Césaire, Damas and Senghor, Dadié and many young intellectuals who
remained in francophone Africa were engaged in creating literature that
evoked African consciousness in an African context. Themes of alienation
and deracination and tones of estrangement, so prevalent in the Negritude
poetry of the period, are strikingly absent in the work of Dadié at the time.

Dadié returned from Dakar in 1947 to the Ivory Coast where he continued to work as a "stringer" for *Le Réveil* and became involved in a struggle
for independence through his work with the *Partie Démocratique de la Côte
d'Ivoire*, the national party that was an off-shoot of the RDA. In February
1949 he was imprisoned until March 1950 along with seven other members
of the Party's Board of Directors. It was from his prison cell that Dadié wrote
his *Carnet de Prison (Prison Diary)*, which was not published until 1980.
Placing the accent on the determination associated with the struggle for
independence voiced in the songs of the political prisoners, Dadié introduces the diary with this entry:

3

The 9th of February in the afternoon, after having paraded us through-out all Abidjan with the perverse intention of demoralizing the militants in a maneuver using old canons and Bren-gun carriers, [in] a deploy-ment of commanding force, a hearse dumped us during the night into Grand Bassam prison. And there we found men who for years had been waiting to be tried...men, a majority of whom were for the most part victims...And we were all there; and everyone, each evening after roll-call, in the locked rooms and cells, sang. They sang in spite of the prison bars, in spite of the Draconian punishment, in spite of hunger...

I hope that this book born in prison gives to the one who will touch it, to the one who will skim it, to the one who will read it, a taste of plenitude, a thirst for freedom and especially a hatred for arbitrariness.[6]

The literature of Dadié is linked strongly to political and social realities in Africa in general and the Ivory Coast in particular. Intensely concerned with creating forums through which African culture and individual talents could find expression, Dadié served as one of the founders and directors of the Theatre Division of the "Cercle Culturel et Folklorique de la Côte d'Ivoire" (Ivory Coast Circle of Culture and Folklore) in 1953. Furthermore, Dadié was "Chef du Cabinet" in the Ministry of National Education in the Ivory Coast after independence, and several years later served as Vice President of UNESCO's (United Nations Educational, Scientific and Cultural Organiza-tion) Executive Council, just two in a long line of official posts he has held. At present, Dadié is Minister of Culture in the Ivory Coast. The various services and responsibilities that the writer has accepted and performed clearly indicate that he views art as an important social necessity.

Having begun his literary career in 1933 with a sketch, *Les Villes (Cities)*, Dadié has shown a continuous propensity through the years for theatrical forms. His twelve plays, though varied in their presentation of themes, focus almost exclusively on some aspect of culture and society. In his *Monsieur Thôgô-Gnini* (1970) Dadié examines the corruption and the adoption of false bourgeois values concommitant with a political system that does not adequately cope with such problems. *Mhoi Cheul (I Alone)* (1979) is an ironic discourse on individuality that when pushed to the extreme becomes eccentric and corruptive. In addition to his work in theatre, Dadié experi-ments with other literary modes. Mention has already been made of the writer's particular handling of the essay between 1936 and 1947. Since that time poetry, short stories, tales and a prison diary have added other dimensions to his literary output. To date, Dadié has published three collec-tions of poetry, *Afrique Debout (Rise Africa)* (1950), *La Rond des Jours (The Succession of Days)* (1956), and *Hommes de tous les Continents (Men*

4

of All Continents) (1967). His four collections of tales and short stories, Légendes Africaines (1954), Le Pagne Noir (The Black Loin Cloth) (1955), Commandant Taureault et ses Nègres (Commander Taureault and his Blacks) (1980), and Les Jambes du fils de Dieu (The Legs of the Son of God) (1980), speak to Dadié's intertextual handling of "orature."

Along with André Terisse, Dadié edited a reading text for use in African primary schools: Les Belles Histoires de Kacou Ananze l'Araignée (The Wonderful Stories of Ananse Kacou the Spider) is designed to teach fundamental reading skills through the use of African tales. In 1953, Dadié published Climbié, a semi-autobiography. This work was Dadié's first major piece of prose and has now been translated into several languages. One of Climbié's distinguishing characteristics is its realistic and unromanticized picture of life in a rural African society during the colonial period. With Un Nègre à Paris (1959), Patron de New York (1964) and La Ville où nul ne meurt (1968), Dadié introduces a new genre into African literature: the "chronique." This especially is an art form that corresponds to a particular historical and social situation in Africa, prior to and following independence from colonial powers.

The term "chronique" (chronicle) usually designates "an historical register or account of facts disposed in the order of time...without philosophic or literary treatment" (OED). Dadié's concept of the chronique, however, does not correspond to that definition. The events depicted in his chroniques are not merely or necessarily disposed in the order of their occurrence. The material which serves as the basis for these works was gathered during two separate trips made by Dadié: one in 1959 to Paris and Rome, and the other in 1964 to New York. None of the works was actually written at the time of the trips. Neither do those dates which appear at the end of each chronique (July 14 - August 2, 1956, for Un Nègre à Paris; March 18, 1963, for Patron de New York; March 24 - April 3, 1959, for La Ville où nul ne meurt [Rome]) correspond to the actual dates of his travels.

A special cosmopolitan view grows out of Dadié's knowledge and understanding of cultures other than his own. He conceives of the chronique as the vehicle for a comparative study of culture which should lead, ideally, to an affirmation of individuality and independence. In La Ville où nul ne meurt Dadié states:

Actually, we don't know how well off we are. You have to travel in order to measure how much distance there is between us and the others...

Some individuals still dare to affirm that traveling educates only young people. It also educates old people, especially when, like me, they have grown up in their sheltered world, worshipped the same god, danced the same dances and walked along the same footpaths that their ances-

5

tors did. What amazement! What an affirmation of the self as an individual and as a nation.[7]

The events of the chronique, rather than being presented in strict chronological order, are arranged according to aesthetic and educational considerations. Those events are selected in retrospect with the purposeful intent of heightening awareness and cultivating an appreciation for the components of one's own culture through critical comparisons and contrasts with similar components of foreign cultures. For Dadié, the chronique as a form expresses his own particular notion of the African's position in the world community. It thus becomes, in his hands, an original literary form that corresponds little to the usual notion of a chronicle.

Dadié's chroniques do not lend themselves to an exclusively deconstructionist criticism where only textual considerations are taken into account. Such an approach can lead neither to a meaningful understanding of the writer's use of the form nor to a full conveyance of its meaning. One must necessarily study the personality out of which the works were born. For the author himself, whether in the form of an assumed persona or an implied narrative voice, is always the principal character in Dadié's chroniques. The reader is called upon to witness a man who has a particular cultural heritage, definite personal philosophies and a certain world view.

Dadié's own relationship to Africa is thus an important element in the chronique. A strong belief in the dynamics of African culture is important to Dadié's thinking. The author insists that casual and outside observers have made hasty and erroneous judgments about African culture and have on occasion dismissed its viability because it is manifested in different ways than is Western culture. In "Le Rôle de la légende dans la culture populaire des noirs d'Afrique," Dadié writes:

> They have neon lighting while we still go by the light of a storm lamp.
> They have the telegraph and we the drum code; they have books and
> we have stories and legends by which our forbears transmitted their
> knowledge. These stories and legends are our museums, monuments
> and street names – our only books, in fact. This is why they have such an
> important place in our lives. Every evening we leaf through them and
> despite the whirl of our present day life, we cling to our past. This gives
> us strength. Over-hasty observers, unaware of these facts, have unfortu-
> nately not always penetrated further than the sordid appearance of our
> straw huts. They have not known how to read the hoary old men sitting
> at the threshold of these straw huts. People with no books, no monu-
> ments, and therefore of no value.[8]

Dadié uses the chronique to redefine and revalorize a cultural ideology based upon his own close contact with traditional elements of African society.

It is through African 'orature,' "that the elders teach the young easily remembered lessons on the cosmogony, tribal history, social laws, origins of their various products, religious beliefs, social structure, economics, relations with other tribes, the lives of the heroes of the fable, the evolution of civilization (that is, invention of the caste system), the foundation of villages, the totemic relationship between an animal and a clan, and above all the cult of friendship carried to such extremes that a lion cub kills its mother to avenge the mother of its human friend."[9] The value of the historical tales and dynastic poems handed down from generation to generation by griots is emphasized by Djibril Tamsir Niane in his preface to *Soundjata ou l'épopée mandingue*:

> Unfortunately, the West has taught us to despise the oral sources of history. Everything that is not written in black and white is considered to be without foundation. There are even plenty of African intellectuals narrow-minded enough to despise these 'talking documents', the griots, and to believe that for lack of written documents we know nothing, or virtually nothing, of our past. Such people simply prove that they know their country only from the white man's point of view. The words of the traditional griots deserve something better than scorn.[10]

Dadié is a kind of modern griot in his handling of the chronique. He uses his extensive knowledge of oral traditions to resurrect various aspects of the African worldview and to adapt them to the twentieth-century world.

It is important, then, that Dadié's ostensible adherence to Christianity, which is shown thematically in much of his literature, be assessed in terms of his traditional education in African philosophies and religions. Dadié identifies his religious persuasion in these words from *La Ville où nul ne meurt*:

> What difference is there between this man next to me and myself? He's Jewish and I'm African; a rabbi, and I'm Roman Catholic. I'm the brother of the Messiah that he gave up to the world...(*The City*, p. 19).

Dadié himself is cogently aware of the parallels, contradictions and ambiguities of his religious eclecticism. He states:

> The new religion thus has an ambiguous function: On the one hand, it

7

assimilates us a little more to the colonizer, but it succeeds in this assimilation because it encounters a spiritual ground which our cosmogonic and theogonic myths have already prepared;...on the other hand, it lightens the burden of our slavery, first of all by the representation it brings us of possible happiness in the afterworld and secondly, by revolutionary ferments, such as the ideas of equality, personal autonomy and fraternity, which it contains.[11]

This religious stance is an example of the process by which, through selection, comparison and integration, Dadié adapts traditional African values to the modern world and fuses the two in a new reality. That process is a characteristic movement in the chronique.

Another basic component of Dadié's ideology expressed in the chronique is a firm belief in human equality. Active political involvement in anti-colonial struggles is an exemplary and tangible manifestation of this conviction. In an article written in 1949, "Le Sens de la Lutte" ("The Meaning of the Struggle") Dadié exposes an essential and representative conviction: "Capitalism is by nature oppressive because it kills in certain individuals every spark of humanity and substitutes for it the most unbearable arrogance and selfishness...France is the Mother Country for subjugated territories, but herself a colony of capitalism."[12] Dadié consistently criticizes all forms of oppression and the very existence of oppressive forces. Such criticism underscores Dadié's dedication to the philosophy of the dignity of all humans and the right of all people and all nations to be free from the violence of imperialism and oppression. This philosophic foundation permeates his chroniques and helps to make them other than mere chronicles of events and happenings.

Dadié's literary output is testimony to his personal philosophy of individual freedom. This has been demonstrated substantively and formally through his literary career. He makes no point of conforming to traditional Western rules of literary conduct. That is to say, he feels no particular allegiance to an already established form of presentation. Moreover, the multi-facetedness of Dadié's artistic output restricts us from labeling or associating him with any particular form. In fact, this controlled and mastered artistic dexterity is one of the characteristics that distinguishes him from other African writers of his generation.

What has motivated Dadié to use such a variety of forms? How does he justify these choices? In an interview the writer reflects:

At school we learnt how to recite eight, ten, twelve (meter) verses. We thought that these classical forms were the only possible ones. This is where I stood. I had something to say but how was I to say it...One day in 1942, I read a free verse poem by Diop Yssa...I said to myself: There are other forms than the classical six, eight, or twelve meter verse...So I tried poems as well as tales and short stories. There is no hierarchy among the various forms of expression, none has precedence over the others. For me, Poetry, Theatre, Short Stories, Chronicles and Tales are simply different methods of working. I accept neither classification nor precedence.[13]

Although Dadie's personal conception of form is a pragmatic one, its literary merits cannot be underestimated. His use of the chronique deserves special attention and study. Its aesthetic relevance, coupled with its political significance, makes this form unique to African literature.

A schematic review of the genres comprising African literatures reveals that the chronique in Dadie's hands is most analogous to African prose fiction in terms of form and structure. Dadie's chroniques are not novels, and, even though important literary parallels do exist, there are definite and distinctive differences. To classify Dadie's chroniques as novels is to place them in a literary category which would void them of their unique qualities.

The body of African prose fiction produced within the last three decades generally corresponds to three periods in African history: the pre-colonial, the colonial and the post-colonial. The distinction among these historical periods should be made, not according to the periods that are portrayed in the works, but according to the writer's attitudes toward the period in which the events in the work take place. For example, in the *traditional* or pre-colonial African novel primary emphasis is placed upon an explanation, and often romanticization, of social and cultural milieux in Africa. The authors of the *colonial* novel view their societies in terms of two basic oppositions: the one between Africa and the West and the other between the old and the new. In the *post-colonial* works authorial points of view are more varied. They portray the replication and differences in relationships of dominance and oppression practiced in colonial and neo-colonial societies. They examine the means for an effective and pragmatic integration of certain traditional African values into the modern African world and they attempt to destroy overly romanticized ideas about African cultures and lifestyles.[14] Many of the basic attitudes toward African society which are present in African prose fiction are to be found in Dadie's chroniques. Through his "reflections on various cultures," the artist skillfully incorporates such attitudes into a new, eclectic vision of reality.

It is noteworthy that several African writers make use of the chronique as a structural device in their novels. Though basic novelistic techniques may vary from one to the other of these writers, the chronique serves as a kind of novelistic substructure for each of them. The chronique is the skeletal framework around which the events in the novels revolve and in relation to which the characters are developed. Mongo Beti's *Le Roi Miraculé* *(King Lazarus)*(1958), subtitled *Chronique des Essazam*, is a case in point. The use of the chronique as a substructure in this novel is evidenced by the fact that the novelistic universe created by Beti is conceived in direct relation to an actual period in African history, more specifically in Cameroonian history, even though the work is entirely fictional. The colonial period, with its chaotic social transitions, is the historical time that is treated. The characters are representative of types found within such a society (the priests, the traditional village leader, the "been to" students, women in polygynous marriages) and the basic conflict opposes traditional values and practices to those held by colonial institutions and their representatives: opposing views of marriage, ethnic allegiances, religious choices, corruption and disruption. From beginning to end, the reader encounters crises faced by individual characters and by the Essazam people as a group. We are led through a certain period in fictional time which corresponds to an actual historical period outside of the novel itself. At the culmination of his narrative, the narrator carefully points up the importance of the chronique as an organizing principle in his fictional world:

> This same week, the tribe dispersed to the four winds, the foreign clansmen went back to their fields and forests, Essazam resumed its usual somnolence; the serious events which this chronique has just related were soon nothing more than a memory.[15]

Ousmane Sembene's *Les Bouts de Bois de Dieu (God's Bits of Wood)* (1962) is another example of the use of the chronique concept as a structural device in fiction. The strike around which the entire fictional work centers corresponds to the Dakar/Niger railway strike in 1947-48. On the one hand Sembene uses the chronique in a conventional way. The actual historical events become the plot in this powerful piece of fiction. Not only does the author situate the action of the novel in the cities where the strike took place, but the general temporal framework which he creates for the novel corresponds to an exact historical moment. However, Sembene moves beyond this traditional concept of the chronique. Within the general temporal and spatial framework of the novel, the notions of chronological time and space are blurred. This blurring is used to emphasize the community and the importance of the collective will in the triumph of the strikers. In spite of the diversity of the characters presented in Sembene's fictional work, individual decisions and actions remain secondary to the collective drive toward economic liberation.

> The question that we must consider here is whether we intend to be responsible for what we have undertaken in the strike. We have made some mistakes, and doubtless we will make others, but is that any reason why we should abandon those who have followed us and trusted us, those who have gone hungry, and those who have been imprisoned or killed?[16]

In this way, Sembene emphasizes the process by which African women and men redefine their social roles in the light of changing economic conditions. Polyrhythmically, the discourse in this novel mirrors and embeds reality in the sense that it chronicles actual events and reflects a significant transitional period in Senegalese society. These novels of Beti and Sembene are two of the most purely literary examples of the use of the chronique in African prose fiction.

With *Le Devoir de Violence (Bound to Violence)* (1968) by Yambo Ouologuem, the chronique is used in yet another way. The novel itself is not a chronique. Rather, the fictional narrative in Chapter One takes the form of an actual representation and analysis of historical events. By thus creating a believable historical reality in the first chapter of the novel, the author makes his development of the historical situations, in the chapters that follow, seem more credible. This historical style reinforces the referential power of the novel. More specifically, it is used to suggest realistic parallels between the historical past and the actual present. The parallels are founded upon information established within the text itself.

Dadié's chroniques were written during crucial moments in his country's historical and social development and span a period of ten years in their dates of publication. Although Dadié uses his own particular cultural background as source material, the experiences and the problems he treats generally reflect those of other people with similar histories. The first chronique, *Un Nègre à Paris*, was published during the colonial period before the French colonial forces were removed from power. The other two, *Patron de New York* and *La Ville où nul ne meurt*, appeared years later during a period of "reconstruction." Colonialism had intrinsically subscribed to exploitation, dehumanization, cultural debasement and political oppression. In addition to the colonized country's natural resources being used for the colonizing country's own economic gains, the foreign governments used their institutions and constitutions to propagate and impose their ideologies upon African peoples. From the perspective of the colonizer, Western culture, with all its social and economic implications, was the superior culture and was upheld as the ideal.

It is this cultural imperialism that Dadié confronts in his chroniques. For Dadié, Western culture is simply one of many cultures and it should neither automatically take precedence over African culture nor be blindly accepted or thought of as being superior. The writer, therefore, uses the chronique in a formal way to undercut an ideological policy of assimilation and mimicry. Dadié emphasizes the belief and the philosophy that one's cultural heritage is not a determinant of superiority. With regard to the social relevance and didacticism of his chroniques, Dadié says:

> It has often been said that such or such a culture is valid, that one is better than another: That is wrong!...Western culture is developed but it is not certain that it has reached its present stage thanks to whites alone...

> As a matter of principle I write to help Africans understand that people have been trying to give them cultural or other complexes. But what is culture? Everyone has culture...People must understand that they are dealing with men, nothing more. At least that is my position as an African writer.[17]

"Universal humanism," as Dadié himself has labeled it, emerges as a recurring value in his chroniques. Humanism means a spiritual view of life where the human rather than the machine is central. Dadié's insistence that human life is of supreme worth and that humans must be treated with dignity and respect and as an end, not as a mere means, is seen throughout his writings and in his chroniques in particular. In these comparative studies of Western and African societies, Dadié extols human dignity which cannot be limited to any particular cultural group or historical era.

Dadié's traditional African education helped him to have an appreciation for the individual as a person and, at the same time, to learn that individualism pushed to the point of egocentricity is a detriment to community living. Persons must be recognized and respected as individuals, but the aggressiveness which can grow out of excessive concern for one's self and for one's own welfare at the expense of concern for others is a destructive and debilitating force in community and group life. Such individualism can lead to the development and acceptance of dehumanizing practices within any given culture. It is no small wonder that Dadié points out the dehumanizing aspects of the various cultures with which he comes in contact and uses these aspects as themes in his writing:

> ...I have been living for the past few years in a society where men who

work themselves to death hardly succeed in making ends meet. Individualism, frantic selfishness, have frightened me throughout my travels. Men who don't even look at each other, neighbors who hardly speak to each other. Cities exist where individuals die from hunger and cold, where neighbors can die and lie undiscovered for months in their room; if by chance in Rome, city of charity, seat of Christianity, of a fraternity that is a bit harrassed throughout the world by the monstrous design of different groups, there were people going in rags, with empty stomachs, scrounging through trash cans and sleeping under bridges, one would have to admit that the world on this side of the ocean is very sick. Christianity having failed in its mission would have to be redesigned on a human scale, that is, brought back to its first principles and not be allowed to be a mere emblem on the doorstep of a civilization that has the most absolute contempt for the individual...(*The City*, p. 20).

This passage shows Dadié's concern for the individual. He rejects the kind of egocentric materialism that destroys purely human values and that is symbolized in *La Ville où nul ne meurt* by the Banco di Santo Spirito, an institution whose very name suggests the transformation of spiritual values into monetary and commercial interests.

Another dehumanizing element of Western culture is the abstraction that characterizes Western thought, Western values, and Western planning. This abstractionism flows from the influence of the philosophy of Descartes whose central notion, the "primacy of consciousness," made its argument in three words: "I think, therefore I am" (Cogito, ergo sum). Descartes explained the world and the soul by mechanical and mathematical laws: "All the world, and every body is a machine..." The Western abstractionism to which Dadié refers is based upon this Cartesian logic, which can divorce people from a natural world and which can make them insensitive to human problems. Dadié points out the mechanistic emphases which have influenced the planning of cities and streets and which have thus stifled and dehumanized:

I'm smothering in these rectangular streets, with no capriciousness, streets drawn by heads and not by hearts, streets that are labeled, made navigable, narrow. I'm smothering in these columns of men hurriedly running from their own work, their own shadows (*The City*, p. 37).

To a certain extent Rome, because of its eternal presence outside of time and its Italian capriciousness, escapes from the pragmatic abstractionism of the West. The butterfly symbolizes the spontaneity and naturalness of life in

13

Rome, for Rome is "a butterfly which has perched itself upon time" (*The City*, p. 124). "The Eternal City, it knows how to blend the lightness, the caprices of the butterfly with the rigorous demands of the modern city" (*The City*), p. 73.

Advertising is seen as yet another dehumanizing aspect of Western culture. Publicity is everywhere. It is symbolized by the huge Cinzano sign at the airport. Advertising dehumanizes because it is a form of propaganda, a kind of brainwashing that leads people to react without thinking and to relinquish their freedom of choice. Advertising is also dehumanizing to the extent that it is an outgrowth of materialistic attitudes that have been carried to the point of inhuman greediness:

> Roma! pronounced as the indigenous people pronounce it...Am I going to find exacerbated here in Rome the selfishness I glimpsed among other peoples? Is man going to be used for the benefit of certain companies just as he is elsewhere? Struggle! Fortune!...Is this really the first lesson that Rome can give me? A chosen people, a first class people, authorized to step on everyone else, in the shadow of the cross? I refuse to believe that of a holy city. And yet, this equatorial blossoming of propaganda boards—made of enamel to withstand the weather—has a deep meaning for me. It is the symptom of a disease, the sign of an attitude, the most obvious indication of a desire for power.
>
> Roma!
>
> Have the merchants who were chased from the original temple found shelter and good land? . . . (*The City*, pp. 64-65).

Advertising represents the egocentrism pushed to the extreme that allows and authorizes Rome, a holy city "in the shadow of the cross," to step on persons in an avid reach for power.

Many of the themes found in the chroniques center around the notions of alienation and community. Alienation, as used in this particular context, has a highly inclusive meaning. On one level, alienation means the observer's physical detachment from his own African society. On another level it means a cultural detachment from the mores, practices, and ideologies of the peoples with whom he is in physical and geographical contact. In certain other cases, the alienation is extended to include the observer's detachment from the environment of which he is physically a part. The latter two forms of alienation are caused by various factors. The causes which are most commonly mentioned are man's disrespect for his fellow man, his false sense of respect for money, and Western man's dependence upon a scientific, rather than a human, approach to life and death. Dadié analyzes this preoccupation with false values:

All means, even the most despicable, are used to bring the enemy to surrender. After having hauled out the gold, the silver, the pearls and the diamonds, they joyously kill old people, women and children. They have here, on this continent, a sovereign contempt for man...

...I'm thinking about...the degradations to which men and women have been submitted...For the person who tortures another, dying doesn't seem to have much significance. Death here is an event that doesn't seem to affect the group as a collective body. Is this why they have such contempt for life and for the individual? . . . (*The City*, p. 43-44).

The same abstractionism which prevents Western man from knowing life and being familiar with death as natural cycles of the cosmic reality is also responsible for his materialism and his disrespect for human values, and is a basic cause of the observer's alienation from Western culture.

Just as the notion of alienation is seen in various levels in the chroniques, so also is the notion of community. Even though the observer is detached physically from his own African society, he retains a definite psychological attachment to it. This psychological attachment is manifested through the conclusions he reaches and the comparisons he makes with various African realities. Community is also evident when the observer draws direct parallels between practices, whether positive or negative, which are present in both the African society he knows and in the foreign society he is visiting. In addition, community is expressed when the observer, even though in a foreign country, feels that he is an integral part of the community he is visiting. And finally, community can be seen among those who are being observed and who share a common cultural heritage.

It is evident, then, that the chronique for Dadié is realistic in conception. It is a form that intentionally deals with the problems raised by a specific historical period. The literary reality found in the chroniques is always based upon actual and non-fictional experiences which Dadié had during his travels. However, because of the manner in which Dadié utilizes, manipulates and resurrects his experiences, he creates the semblance of a fictional reality. One of the most important characteristics of the chronique, as it is used by Dadié, is this alliance of a basic, substantive realism with literary, fictional techniques within the same work. In the chronique, Dadié uses the literary techniques of the persona and the implied narrator, of irony, of specific techniques for augmenting the referential power of the chronique, of associative narration, of specific descriptive effects and of thematic arrangements.

As the reader travels through Paris, New York and Rome, through the medium of the chroniques, he, together with the narrator, is in touch with a certain African reality. This feeling of proximity to an African experience emanates from the presence of that African personality which is ever-permeating and ubiquitous, which is almost omnipresent. There is always but one central personality in the chroniques. That personality has a veiled identity, but the reader senses that the voice is that of Dadié himself. In a certain sense, the author dons the mask of an integrated African personality, the unity of whose experiences, disposition, philosophy and system of values makes him an identifiable persona. This persona is identifiable to the extent that he exemplifies an ideal African personality who is a microcosm of the traditional African and in whom are integrated and summed up the most important aspects of the African personality. That the voice of Dadié speaks through the persona, is confirmed by the writer:

> In all these works, there is no imagined character whom we can follow throughout the adventures and ups and downs of his life. To the contrary, this is a real character, always myself, who looks, who examines the customs, mores, the culture of a people (French, Italian, American) and (who) judges relative to the customs, mores and culture of my people, in an effort to discern the differences and the points of community in the perspective of universal humanism.[18]

Such narrative proximity between Dadié and the persona necessarily colors and structures the approach which is used. But much more important is the fact that Dadié introduces a particularly authentic kind of personalization into African literature.

In *Un Nègre à Paris*, the first of Dadié's chroniques to be published, the writer's narrative approach is explicitly expressed at the beginning of the text, just prior to the departure for Paris. This chronique is semi-epistolary in form in that it consists of one letter written by Tanhoe Bertin to an African friend. The letter begins:

> Leaving with the eyes of all of my friends, of all of my relatives, leaving with their nose in order to smell Paris' air, with their feet in order to tread in Paris' soil...I will be no one's tributary. No one will see for me, no one will think for me. I'll go to the adventure, and I will look...I'll look for me, for you, for all of us.[19]

With this statement the narrator immediately establishes the frame of reference which will be used by the persona through the voice of the narrator. Dadié thus exposes in his first chronique the modus operandi which will be used in each of the other two. Though it is not explicitly stated at the beginning of the other two chroniques, the technique remains the same.

The psychological nature of the persona presented in these works is significant. In *La Révolte des romanciers noirs de langue française (The Revolt of Black Novelists of French Expression)*, Jingira Archiriga most accurately and concisely describes the Dadié persona as "un Nègre sans complexe," a black without complexes.[20] Even though Archiriga is referring specifically to the persona in *Un Nègre à Paris*, his description is equally applicable to the persona in Dadié's other two chroniques. Dadié, as persona and implied narrator, is presented as self-confident, self-assured and as having a strong identity as well as pride in his own African culture. The significance of a persona with these attributes lies in the fact that it assures, to a great extent, authorial independence. Some Africans find themselves so spiritually displaced in the Western city that they often begin to question their own identities. Such is the case with Samba Diallo, the central character in Kane's *Aventure Ambigüe*, who undergoes a serious identity crisis in Paris, after having left his home in Senegal. It is precisely Dadié's self-assurance, his confidence in himself and his pride in his own African society and culture which give him the freedom and the authorial independence and courage to search for and to find points of community between his African society and the various Western societies. It is this kind of self-assurance which allows him to compare, and often to criticize, both his own and foreign societies as he does in the following passage from *La Ville où nul ne meurt*:

> These men, with their sometimes cramped gestures, have organized their existence in such a way that our life is more intimate behind the bamboo fixings of our undecorated straw houses, behind our dried clay walls with no gilted ceilings.
>
> Our contempt for gold has undoubtedly saved us from dangerous tropisms. To us, the eyes of our fellow men don't yet appear as escarbuncles, diamonds or other precious stones to be pulled out; and their sweat as fertile manure for sterile lands, or first choice oil for rusty machines. In this regard, we can still be placed in the flattering category of a young people. A youth that will pass quickly if ever one day we enter into contact with the people from here; and it is even to be feared that we'll beat them in the rush for gold, trampling everything underfoot, including our own children (*The City*, p. 52).

The persona, without complexes and without prejudices, moves easily beyond questions of national identity and race to the potential for greed and materialism that is so apparent in parts of Europe and Africa alike.

Dadié's authorial independence is also seen as he describes an African acquaintance who has been spiritually displaced in his own African country because of Western influence. The rejection of African culture made by this African acquaintance is not one of which he is aware. It is not a conscious rejection, but rather a displacement of his own traditional African values by his acceptance of Western ideas. In *Patron de New York*, Dadié describes an experience en route from his home in Abidjan to New York. The plane makes a stop, which presumably is Dakar. During the wait in Dakar, Dadié makes an attempt to telephone some of his friends and acquaintances in governmental positions. None of them can be reached. But in response to the narrator's inquiry as to where one of these acquaintances is, the secretary replies that he is "en métropole." Further inquiry by the narrator reveals that this friend is in Paris. The "métropole" is thus considered as the "people's center," as the hub around which revolve the most important aspects of the people's lives. In his acceptance of Paris as the "métropole," the narrator's friend is relegating the African city of Dakar to the inferior status of some relatively unimportant satellite of Paris. It is the attributing of this inferior status to his own African place of residence which reveals the extent to which the shackles imposed by the teachings and influence of Western culture still bind this man's mind and his sense of self-worth. The narrator responds to the message saying: "France has really marked the heart and mentality of its former subjects."[21]

In spite of Dadié's authorial independence, the single voice which emanates from the persona raises the very basic literary question of authorial objectivity and subjectivity. Even though the narrator and the persona are one, confident and controlled, one does have the distinct impression of objectivity. Through the use of certain narrative techniques, the objectivity comes to the surface. In *Un Nègre à Paris*, for example, the narrator is named Tanhoe Bertin. This naming of the character is a vehicle for personalization, a technique which distances the author from the character and gives the reader the impression that the author is not equivalent to the persona.

In the two chroniques *Patron de New York* and *La Ville où nul ne meurt*, the objectivity is expressed more in terms of style and other forms of narrative distancing. For example, in *Patron de New York* during the period that the airplane is en route to New York, the narrator speaks for any non-English speaking person and not for himself in particular. The narrator's speech is not an expression limited by his own experiences and prejudices, but articulates an idea which would allow any non-American and/or non-English speaker to find points of identification and sympathy. After the flight attendant, speaking only in the English language, has made announcements over the intercom system relative to important safety instructions of which each passenger should be aware, the narrator satirically remarks that the deaths of non-American passengers would obviously not be a catastrophy. This comment takes on a social significance which is broad and not limited solely to the perspective of an African person. Narrative distancing is also evident in *La Ville où nul ne meurt*. A case in point is where Dadié refers to his country as "that country" instead of "my country." By use of this narrative distancing, the writer makes a technical distinction between his personal observations and his observations as an objective observer.

To observe the interaction between a people and an environment, to study the ostensible effects of this environment upon the people and then to report with fidelity what one sees is objectivity. Such reporting is done from the stance of an outsider looking in: it corresponds to the role of the uninvolved clinician who records "what he sees" without involving his own prejudices or examining the dynamics of "why he sees." The reporter who is subjective, on the other hand, may be a physical part of and a participant within the environment. He transcends that environment which surrounds him, looks back at himself as an object within the environment and then proceeds to interpret his feelings as participant. The subjective reporter knows the fears, the ideas and the motivating forces of the participant within an environment. In Dadié's chroniques we sometimes witness an objective reporter and at other times we see a subjective one.

It is at that point where we can recognize the two types of reporters, working as a single unit, that the writer's literary dexterity is at its best. Of the three chroniques this duality of reporting is more completely developed in *La Ville où nul ne meurt* and *Un Nègre à Paris*. In the narrator's prolonged observation and analytical description of the rabbi in the former chronique the coupling of both objective and subjective reporting is readily seen. The observer first encounters the rabbi on a bus which is transporting passengers from the center of Paris to Orly Airport. Initially the rabbi is described in these words:

> In the bus that takes us away towards Orly, on the seats to the left, an old, bearded man, dressed in black...Unctuous, calculated, ponderous gestures...His hands have the twitches characteristic of individuals who reign over thousands of consciences. They rub together, join together, cross each other, open, close.

Then the reporter's subjectivity enters into this description when he adds:

> A truly happy man, confident in himself, in the future, safe from every storm, one of those upon whom it is difficult to cast any doubt...I bet that he's found the road that leads straight to paradise (*The City*, pp. 41-42).

The author reports objectively on the rabbi's gestures and physical characteristics when he describes those traits and qualities that can be identified from
sensory observation and experience. Subjectivity enters when he takes the
data resulting from his sensory observations and experiences and attempts to
interpret what he has seen.

In the example from *Un Nègre à Paris*, the reader becomes more actively
engaged in the narrator's movement from the objective to the subjective:

> When you come to Paris, this Paris which lives underground circulating
> in the subway, buy yourself a guide as soon as possible...Then get a sub-
> way map. Armed with this map get lost in the labyrinth of corridors and
> arrows, of direction signs and rushing humans, of one ways, of ups (this
> way) and downs (that way), let the subway leave that you should have
> taken and take the one that you shouldn't have, then get off at a station
> somewhere, walk out, walk back in, take shelter against the ticket
> punching machine and explain to it that you've gone in the wrong direc-
> ection, leave again, get lost again, and finally go out, take the boulevard
> and go straight ahead. It's only on these terms that you can call yourself
> Parisian. This is to say that you will have understood the meaning of
> arrows, the corridors, the language of pointing fingers.[22]

The first two and the last two sentences of this passage represent the
narrator's attempt at objectivity. He plays the role of the concerned and
experienced guide who carefully leads us with definite, precise instructions
into the subway. In the end, the narrator is able to determine the conditions
necessary for our being able to cope with that "iron god" which is so much a
part of Parisian life. It is during the actual trip on the subway itself and during
the moments of movement into and out of the subway station that we enter
into a vicarious experience with the narrator. We go where he has already
been; we see what he has already seen. In a sense we begin to learn what he
has already known. His personal, intimate and subjective experiences
become our own.

Ironic narration is the primary technique used by Dadié to underscore
the persona's objective and subjective reporting. Irony, in a very narrow
definition of the term, is a figure of speech in which the idea intended to be
conveyed is different from, usually the opposite of, the literal meaning of
the words used. In its broad sense, irony is a conflict between reality and
appearance. It is in the broad sense of the term that Dadié uses ironic narration to show the conflict between the professed and the practiced, between
the pronouncements and the actual use or non-use of those announced
beliefs in social behavior. When explaining the historical significance of the

Roman Square, Piazza dei Cinquecento, the narrator says:

> According to history, Rome, forgetting that she had aged, and thus misjudging her powers, got into a dispute with an African nation over something trifling: a few acres of land. Elders are sometimes aggressive, the last stand against decrepitude. Rome undoubtedly scorned the wise advice that her neighbors didn't hesitate to offer. On the first day of conflict, she lost five hundred fighters, five hundred new heroes. Men who, while still alive, were dying probably from hunger. Now the nation cherished them. A disaster, a national shame; that this calamity could happen when they were attacking a well armed European nation can be understood, but that it should be inflicted by a somewhat unsophisticated tribe seemed strange (*The City*, pp. 76-77).

In Dadié's use of the ironic narrative technique the conflict is hidden from those participating in the events with whom the narrator comes into contact, but it is clearly seen by the reader. This ironic narration is extended as the narrator employs Socratic irony by pretending to adopt the Westerners' point of view on certain issues for the purpose of ridiculing the Western audience. In both examples of ironic narration, the specific references which are made are not in themselves visibly ironic; the ironic quality of the statements is attributed to them by the reader as he interprets and infers. The persona succeeds in his ironic narration because he is able to understand two points of view. Ironic narration is used to make inquiry into the conduct of others. It is also used to invite others to make even deeper inquiries into their own conduct.

Although the chronique is basically realistic in thrust and concerned with specific realities outside the work itself, Dadié must necessarily make use of techniques that will allow him to communicate his vision adequately. Thus, the "referential power" of the chronique is another of its fundamental literary characteristics. An individual is able to understand and comprehend when the ability to reason by analogy and inference is possessed. Both inductive and deductive reasoning require knowledge of a particular experience before that experience can be related to a general or different one. As Dadié describes a particular experience with which his readers can identify, a relationship is established between the readers' personal experiences and those recounted in the chroniques. Dadié's ability to relate events in a manner which allows the reader to make inferences and deductions that go beyond the reality of the work itself is what constitutes the "referential power" of the chronique.

In a discussion about the French general who regained power and renamed himself Napoleon, the narrator remarks: "I thought that only men from home changed names when changing conditions" (*The City*, p. 60). When the narrator talks of how the word "Caesar" means elephant he asks: "Don't we have the elephant as an emblem? Don't our sovereigns call themselves elephants in order to give themselves more weight? To call one-self Lion, Tiger, Leopard, Elephant and then to maintain that man is superior to animals seems like an aberration to me" (*The City*, p. 80). Through the chronique's referential power, the narrator is better able to achieve realistic cultural comparisons. Embedded in the texts of the chroniques are specific references to the Ivory Coast as a nation. These comparisons, in turn, result in the development of heightened awareness and the achievement of those social goals which the author wants his works to fulfill, and his audience to understand.

The manner in which references are displayed in Dadié's chroniques underscores another particular stylistic quality. His is a discursive presentation. The specific references made and the parallels drawn serve as catalystic agents in a deductive and associative relationship. Dadié employs a type of involuntary recall where a specific personal encounter on the part of the observer often initiates a deepening of thought or the raising of important social or cultural questions. For example, in *Patron de New York* the recognition of the American flag stimulates a discussion on the history of slavery in America. The narrator reveals a cogent awareness of the important role Black Americans have played in the building of America. The passage ends with the following statement:

> The black man carries the weight of all the stars from the American banner. A black star is certainly missing in this flag. To put one there will be the only permanent way of reminding everyone that there are American blacks on this continent also having freedom.[23]

The reader is presented with a culturally and socially significant commentary on Black nationalism. However, the narrator says nothing more; he makes no attempt at explanation; he moves on unobtrusively to another reference. Through this process, the reader is called upon to assume an active role in the reading of the text. Still he must reflect upon what the observer has said and relate that to personal views of history and society.

It is the association of the observer's experiences with similar ones on the part of the reader which substantiates the chroniques' referential power. Gordon Allport has stated:

> Any experience...in another organism can be inferred from structure, history, and behavior only when a similar experience...has been asso-

ciated...; and the probability of the inference will be proportional to the degree of similarity.[24]

Each of Dadié's three chroniques is comprised of a series of such references. Moreover, it is noteworthy that these references serve as a nucleus for thematic treatments. Though the degree to which the themes are developed may vary from one chronique to the other, the presentation process is basically the same in each. In *La Ville où nul ne meurt* and in *Un Nègre à Paris*, however, these themes are tightly interwoven into the narratives. This is to say that the referential stories which the observer constantly uses are closely related to his journeys throughout the cities. On the other hand, in *Patron de New York*, one has the clear impression that the references are more arbitrary. There is very little notion of spontaneity, leaving one with the idea that the narrator's remarks were premeditated. It is in this regard that *Patron de New York* differs stylistically from the other two chroniques.

The reader is encouraged in the process of association and inference because that movement characterizes the narrator's own attitude toward reality. He refuses to let rigorous cartesian logic and discipline impede the spontaneity he brings to his search for understanding. Thus, the logical, sequential order of the chronique is destroyed as the narrator carries us along by using a technique that one could call "associative narration." Any objective phenomenon can serve as the point of departure for long digressions on the part of the narrator. Thus, in the bus on the way to Orly in *La Ville où nul ne meurt*, we move quickly and spontaneously through the discussion of subjects as varied as the concentration camps and the persecution of the Jews in World War II, the black princes in Paris, the past racial injustices in Western nations, the possibility of future revolutions and the world of tomorrow as it will be seen by the youth of today (*The City*, pp. 41-46). The narration has its own internal logic. It is set off by the vision of the rabbi in the bus and the limping black man glimpsed as the bus passed by. The passage is held together by the thread running through it, the idea of oppression in all its varied forms. The narration moves about easily in time and space, transcends time and space to better grasp the human problems involved.

Dadié is a master of dramatic description, a technique that often entails the personification of inanimate objects. For example, in *La Ville où nul ne meurt*, the narrator describes his inability to master the Roman technique of eating pasta in the following way:

In a very friendly manner, they had told me over and over again how to prevent my mistakes: 'it's very simple; look; plunge your fork in the pile of pasta then turn the fork around several times and you've got it!' I never succeeded. I plunged my fork in the pile, right in the middle, turned, turned, turned, but each time, as if to defy me, a rebellious pasta unwound just at the moment I stuck my mouth out like a bulldozer ready to scoop up its mouthful of sand; this rebellious and unsociable pasta, bent on embarrassing me, had to fall on the napkin in spite of my discreet efforts to put it back on the plate (*The City*, p. 82).

The use of the dramatic description serves two purposes here. On the one hand, it is used to create the light-hearted and humorous tone that is characteristic of Dadié, even when he is treating serious issues of rather great importance. On the other hand, the event, precisely because it is exaggerated out of all proportion and thus underlined, serves to emphasize the narrator's inability to feel completely at home in the Italian city. In either case the dramatic description helps to create the semblance of a fictional reality because it transforms everyday objects and actions and presents them in a new light to the reader.

The personified pasta is only one of the many examples of objects that take on an independent and autonomous existence in Dadié's works. The narrator/observer in the chroniques seems intent upon fully grasping the most minute details of the reality around him in order to better understand the culture he is observing. At other times this myopic approach to description seems to recreate the animated natural world of traditional Africa:

The Roman rain, most certainly curious or mischievous, was revoltingly impolite. It made a real drum out of my nose. My nostrils, revolted, spread with rage. Such a revolt having never been seen in Rome before, the rain got offended: Black nostrils raring up under a caress! Come on! At that precise moment, another little burst of thunder. War was declared. I held out the back of my right hand, she beat it violently (*The City*, p. 100).

At still other moments, Dadié creates objects and realities out of words. A favorite technique of his is to reduce idiomatic expressions to their literal meaning, thus transforming the reality around him. For instance, in speaking of the Parisian workers, he uses the expression "marcher au pas" (to walk in step) to describe the workers' mechanical and inhuman attitudes. The "steps" of the workers become the innumerable feet of centipedes; the workers themselves become a herd with only one head, one body, and thousands of feet. Dadié continues:

But can a foot think? And the paradox is that here men spend enormous sums to teach their children to think. Can you think when you're a foot? Puzzling; the sheep who leaves the herd has an advantage over man: he only has four feet (*The City*, p. 98).

Through myopic description and the reduction of an idiomatic expression to its literal meaning, Dadié has created a new reality: an ugly, technological, human sheep with centipede feet. That reality is used to convey the unthinking and inhuman plight of the Parisian worker. Such descriptive effects are seen as well in *Un Nègre à Paris* and *Patron de New York*, and represent an important aesthetic component of the chronique.

In *La Ville où nul ne meurt*, by a process that can be called "selectivism," Dadié isolates objects from everyday reality, exaggerates their importance through repetition and emphasis, and thus turns them into symbols. Mention has already been made of the Banco di Santo Spirito and the Cinzano sign. Both are cited repeatedly. The first becomes symbolic of the usurpation of the spiritual by the material and the commercial, a process that appears characteristic to Dadié: "It's in these countries that I have understood to what extent wealth can divide men, put them at odds with each other, make them aggressive and inhuman. Undoubtedly it isn't by accident that Jesus was born here in the direst of poverty" (*The City*, p. 121). Dadié is probably ironic when he states that the Romans have tried to counteract the harmful effects of money by placing "it under the power of the Holy Spirit" (*The City*, p. 81). Of the Cinzano sign, Dadié writes: "It is the symptom of a disease, the sign of an attitude, the most obvious indication of a desire for power" (*The City*, p. 65). Like all advertising, the Cinzano and Coca Cola signs are a means of controlling the minds of men: "To consume the same beverage is to acquire the same modes of thought... Coca Cola unites continents which march briskly toward the 'Coca Cola civilization' " (*The City*, p. 102).

The symbolic value of the Roman ruins is less obvious at first glance. The ruins take their significance from their close association with the notion of time passing: "These statues! debris of creation that one would have wanted to be permanent and which time disjoints! They were asked to magnify a reign, a history, to be its heralds. There they are crumbling into dust" (*The City*, p. 104). The disintegration in time that the ruins demonstrate makes one more aware of the limits of men and their actions: "Here human vanity bursts forth" (*The City*, p. 107). The awareness of man's limitations and the essential unimportance of his activities are obscured in the pragmatic time of the everyday world where people are turned into machines in constant motion:

The Parisian who has been told by all the manuals that time is money, that he must know how to make use of it, that he mustn't waste it, is very shocked to see the Roman waiting for him on a cafe terrace or on a garden bench. Thus the awareness grows inside him. He discovers the most terrible of frauds: that men have cut time up for him into hours, minutes and seconds. He understands why he wears a number in the factory (*The City*, p. 97).

In Rome, the presence of the crumbling ruins makes the vanity of human activity evident. The ruins allow men to live outside of pragmatic time and to understand what is essentially and eternally human: "...everything here seems to be filled with real humanity. The men attempt to break away from the flow of time in order to chat joyously on her shores" (*The City*, p. 119).

The butterfly is closely associated with the ruins in its symbolic significance. The butterfly first appears on an advertisement seen at the airport (*The City*, p. 73). It occurs again in the "Song of the Butterfly" that the narrator hears in a restaurant: "Delicate butterfly, colored butterfly, white and yellow butterfly, it is the flower of the sky and the star of God the Father" (*The City*, p. 123). The butterfly is associated with the delicate and the poetic, with spirituality and with leisurely dreaming: "Rome knows how to dream, how to put men at ease. Rome invites you to flutter" (*The City*, p. 73). Above all, the butterfly is associated with the eternally human, discovered beyond pragmatic materialism and harried, everyday reality.

The thematic arrangements that we have alluded to in *Un Nègre à Paris* and *La Ville où nul ne meurt* constitute in and of themselves a literary technique. In theory, the events of the chronicle should be selected and arranged according to the demands of chronological development alone. It is apparent, however, that Dadié chooses and places events in such a way as to bring out important themes. Examples are the notion of universal humanism and its corollary, the notion of dehumanization, or the various forms of alienation and community. Such thematic arrangement is most evident in *La Ville où nul ne meurt* where, through the process of selectivism that we have just discussed, Dadié is able to transform objects into symbols around which the principal themes are developed. The theme of dehumanization through materialism, the supplanting of spiritual values by commercial interests, is emphasized in various situations throughout the work and is crystalized in the four symbolic objects. Indeed, the struggle between materialistic and spiritual values constitutes the very structure of the work:

The Rome of Popes! Why does everyone ask me if I've ever seen the Pope? I understand the meaning of the struggles that two forms of civilization are fighting here. The first, static, dreaming of privileges; made for clients or stockholders in the Bank of the Holy Spirit or the Bank of Rome. The second, dynamic, wants to teach man to think less about his stomach and his skin. It upsets the old vision that makes up the strength of a world, of a continent. It undermines what one could call 'europocentrism' (*The City*, p. 131).

Every situation in *La Ville où nul ne meurt* is presented so as to enhance and emphasize this struggle. The joy of Rome, for Dadié, is that in the Eternal City spiritual values win out over materialism. That triumph is communicated through the various references to the four symbolic objects: the Banco di Santo Spirito, the Cinzano sign, the ruins and the butterfly. The latter two objects win out in Rome and take precedence over the first two. The dehumanization of commercialism is, if not conquered, at least controlled by the ability of the Romans to live outside time, beyond pragmatic concerns, in order to dream, to appreciate the poetic, the spontaneously natural and the human: "This is Rome! A butterfly which has perched itself upon time" (*The City*, p. 124). And, "How can you die when you are perched upon time" (*The City*, p. 134)? Rome is the city where no one dies because the Romans, through their understanding of the ruins and their fascination with the butterfly, are able to transcend the material and the pragmatic and to rise to the level of the purely human. It is this aspect of life that Dadié would like to remain in his new African nation.

Through the chroniques, Dadié has with integrity sought to raise levels of consciousness during a period in history when African culture and institutions have been denigrated by colonialism. By exploring the history and the actual practices of peoples in foreign settings, the writer revealingly exposes the fact that all people share common problems and that at the same time, history and culture account for differences. Through the referential power of his works and through ironic narration, the nonsense of Western society's claim to cultural superiority is reified. Thus, Dadié's writing, like the African writing of the time, is also protest literature. Through the cultural comparative studies afforded by his chroniques, he censures those who have sought to give Africans a low sense of their own personal worth, and gives a new and deserved sense of dignity, self-identity and self-awareness to those with an African cultural heritage. Dadié's willingness to make protests and to speak out against tyranny and oppression of all kinds, his willingness to suffer imprisonment for publicly stating these beliefs in the newspaper, is a very clear indication that he felt some responsibility for the conditions of human life. Though he did not foster or participate in the actions that led to some of the miserable aspects of life in the colonized African country, he accepted some responsibility by using his art, his influence, and his efforts to effect change.

Dadié's chroniques are not protests alone, however, nor are they solely a celebration of his African culture. They are vehicles of instruction. These chroniques encourage the appreciation of those qualities in all cultures, whether Western or African, which will lend themselves to the conservation and enhancement of human life. At the same time and through the same vehicles Dadié rejects and calls upon his readers to reject those things within various cultures which dehumanize and bring misery to the human condition.

...I think about the war in spite of myself. When the animal in man has risen up, must he at all times and all places hang his head?

In the name of what and why do people still make war? Is it to show that, as authentic descendants of old warriors, they don't intend to abandon any of their ancestral practices? It's an extreme pleasure for them to destroy the nettles in the Celestine fields: and the nettles are the men who have another color, another language, other customs. Often it's your neighbor.

They no longer know how to make room for a neighbor because they no longer have real, close ties with what surrounds them. Everyone here is placed on a pedestal from where he looks at other creatures. And because he is on his pedestal, he wants others to pay him homage (*The City*, pp. 61-62).

The three chroniques by Bernard Dadié, *Un Nègre à Paris, Patron de New York* and *La Ville où nul ne meurt* reflect an original and well defined aesthetic. Dadié introduces a new kind of characterization into African literature: the masked persona. He displays an unusual ability to incorporate a didactic quality in his writings by complementing creative genius with thematic treatments. In retrospect Dadié selects certain events and gives the reader the illusion that the events are being disposed in the order of time. He deliberately and artistically transforms his experiences through his use of the persona and the implied narrator, of irony, of specific techniques for augmenting the referential power of the chronique, of associative narration, of specific descriptive effects and thematic arrangements. Throughout these chroniques, Dadié has relied upon his knowledge of religious and cultural histories, and his belief in the dynamics of his African culture in the objectification of subjective experiences.

Dadié's chroniques added new social and cultural dimensions to African writings. Through the chroniques, we see a sensitive, aware and deeply spiritual artist who is at once effective, dynamic and comfortable with his work. Dadié is at home with his particular stylistic presentation because it is an almost direct reflection of his character. He respects tradition and at the same time ventures into new areas of thought through the use of a medium which can be used to express that which he feels obligated to share. Dadié and his chroniques are woven together; they co-exist in a symbiotic relationship. The writer's use of the form underscores his own cultural pride and at the same time emphasizes his shaping of a new discourse in the canon of African literature. In effect, Dadié has used a medium which has not previously been an accepted literary genre for African writing.

Translator's Note

I have purposely kept the translation of *La Ville où nul ne meurt* as literal as possible. There were some problems, however, and when the text was changed I made note of that. An explanation for each change is made in the "Notes on Translation" to be found at the end of the text. I hope that this translation will help to expand the study of African literatures and to encourage critical discourse. My translation is based on the Présence Africaine edition of *La Ville où nul ne meurt (Rome)*, Paris, 1968, the only extant published text.

Janis A. Mayes
Syracuse University
June 1985

NOTES

¹Some of the research for this introduction is based on a series of interviews I had with Bernard Dadié between 1978 and 1980 while I was a Fulbright Scholar at The National University of Ivory Coast. A portion of the introduction has been discussed in my article, "Bernard Dadié and the Aesthetics of the Chronique: An Affirmation of Cultural Identity," *Présence Africaine* 101 - 102 (1977), pp. 102 - 118. For a thorough discussion of the meaning of N'Zima, refer to B. Kotchy, *La Critique sociale dans l'oeuvre théatrale de Bernard Dadié* (Paris: Harmattan), p. 29.

² Richard Bonneau, *Ecrivains, cinéastes et artistes ivoriens* (Abidjan: Les Nouvelles Editions Africaines, 1974), p. 42.

³Janis A. Mayes, Interview with Bernard Dadié, January 14, 1975, Abidjan, Ivory Coast.

⁴Claude Quillateau, *Bernard Binlin Dadié: l'homme et l'oeuvre* (Paris: Présence Africaine, 1967), pp. 12-13. Translations from this work are my own.

⁵Ibid, p. 141.

⁶Bernard Dadié, *Carnet de Prison* (Abidjan: CEDA, 1980), p. 15. Translation my own.

⁷Bernard Dadié, *The City Where No One Dies*, trans. Janis A. Mayes, p. 79. All subsequent references to this translation will be indicated by the abbreviation *The City*, followed by the appropriate page number in the text.

⁸Bernard Dadié, "Le Rôle de la légende dans la culture populaire des noirs d'Afrique," *Présence Africaine*, 14-15 (1957), 165. Cited in Claude Wauthier, *The Literature and Thought of Modern Africa: A Survey*, trans., Shirley Kay (London: Pall Mall Press, 1966), p. 67.

⁹Ibid.

[10]Djibril Tamsir Niane, *Sundiata: An Epic of Old Mali*, trans. G.D. Picket (London: Longmans, 1965), p. viii.

[11]Claude Quillateau, *Bernard Binlin Dadié: l'homme et l'oeuvre* (Paris: Présence Africaine, 1967), p. 147.

[12]Bernard Dadié, "Le Sens de la lutte," *Le Réveil*, 14 February 1949, p. 1, col. 3 and p. 3, col. 2.

[13]Richard Bonneau, "Bernard Binlin Dadié, écrivain ivorien," *Entente Africaine*, 10 (1972), p. 54.

[14]These categories are generally used in criticism on the African novel. Some critics use the term "protest literature" to describe the colonial period literature. Although these three categories are generally used, the definitions that I develop for them in the introduction are my own.

[15]Mongo Beti, *Le Roi miraculé: chronique des Essazam* (Paris: Buchet/Chastel, 1958), p. 250. In the existing English version of this novel (*King Lazarus*, Paris: Frederick Muller, 1960), the passage is not translated in the same way:

> That same week, the tribe was dispersed to the four winds once more. The upcountry clans went back to their fields and forests; Essazam regained its usual somnolent calm and very soon the grave incidents were no more than a memory. (*King Lazarus*, p. 188).

The translation is unfortunate in that it tends more toward interpretation than translation. Beti's ideas and most certainly the concept which he has of his own work must necessarily be left intact.

[16]Sembene Ousmane, *God's Bits of Wood* (New York: Doubleday and Co., 1962), p. 240.

[17]Richard Bonneau, "Bernard Binlin Dadié, écrivain ivorien," *Entente Africaine*, 10 (1972), 57.

[18]Claude Quillateau, *Bernard Binlin Dadié: l'homme et l'oeuvre* (Paris: Présence Africaine, 1967), p. 152.

[19]Bernard Dadié, *Un Nègre à Paris* (Paris: Présence Africaine, 1959), p. 9-10. All translations from this text are my own.

[20]Jingira Archiriga, *La Révolte des romanciers noirs de langue française* (Ottawa: Editions Naaman, 1973), p. 153.

[21]Bernard Dadié, *Patron de New York* (Paris: Présence Africaine, 1964), pp. 11-12. The translations from this text are my own.

[22]Bernard Dadié, *Un Nègre à Paris* (Paris: Présence Africaine, 1959), p. 55.

[23]Bernard Dadié, *Patron de New York* (Paris: Présence Africaine, 1964),

p. 38.

[24]Gordon Allport, *Personality: An Interpretation* (New York: Henry Holt and Co., 1937), p. 524.

BIBLIOGRAPHY

Ade-Ojo, S. "L'Ecrivain africain et ses publics: le cas de Bernard Dadié." *Peuples noirs/Peuples Africains,* 32 (1983), pp. 64-97.

Allport, Gordon. *Personality: An Interpretation.* New York: Henry Holt and Co., 1937.

Archiriga, Jingira J. *La Révolte des romanciers noirs de langue française.* Ottawa: Editions Naaman, 1973.

Beti, Mongo. *King Lazarus.* New York: Macmillan, 1971. Translation of *Le Roi Miraculé.*

——————. *Le Roi miraculé: chronique des Essazam.* Paris: Buchet/Chastel, 1958.

Bonneau, Richard. "Bernard Binlin Dadié, écrivain ivorien." *Entente Africaine,* 10 (1972), 52-57.

——————. *Ecrivains, cinéastes et artistes ivoriens.* Abidjan: Les Nouvelles Editions Africaines, 1974.

Closets D'Errey, Henride. *Proverbes et Idiotismes Français-Anglais.* Paris: Pondichery, 1939.

Cornevin, Robert. "La Littérature ivorienne et Bernard Dadié." *France-Eurafrique,* 180 (1967), 35-43.

Crowder, Michael. *West Africa Under Colonial Rule.* Evanston: Northwestern University Press, 1968.

Dadié, Bernard. *Afrique debout.* Paris: Seghers, 1953.

——————. *Beatrice du Congo.* Paris: Présence Africaine, 1970.

——————. *Carnet du prison.* Abidjan: CEDA, 1980.

——————. *Climbié.* Paris: Seghers, 1953.

——————. *Commandant Taureault et ses nègres.* Abidjan: CEDA, 1980.

——————. *Hommes de tous les continents.* Paris: Présence Africaine, 1967.

——————. *Iles de Tempête.* Paris: Présence Africaine, 1973.

——————. *La Ronde des jours.* Paris: Seghers, 1956.

——————. *La Ville où nul ne meurt (Rome).* Paris: Présence Africaine, 1968.

_____. *Le Pagne noir*. Paris: Présence Africaine, 1955.

_____."Le Rôle de la légende dans la culture populaire des noirs d'Afrique," *Présence Africaine*, 14-15, 1957.

_____."Le Sens de la lutte." *Le Réveil,* 4 April 1949, p. 3, cols. 2-3.

_____. *Légendes africaines.* Paris: Seghers, 1954.

_____. *Les Jambes du fils de Dieu.* CEDA-Hatier, 1980.

_____. *Les Voix dans le vent.* Editions CLE, 1970.

_____. "Leurs hommes." *Le Réveil*, 6 March 1949, p. 1, col. 3, and p. 3, col. 2.

_____. *Mhoi Cheul*. Paris: Présence Africaine, 1979.

_____. *Min-Adjao: Théatre populaire en République de la Côte d'Ivoire (oeuvres choisies).* Abidjan: Centre Cultural de la Côte d'Ivoire, 1965. p. 91-110.

_____. *Monsieur Thôgô-Gnini.* Paris: Présence Africaine, 1970.

_____. "Nous Maintiendrons." *Le Réveil*, 17 January 1949, p. 3.

_____. *Papa Sidi, Maître Escroc.* Dakar: NEA, 1975.

_____. *Patron de New York.* Paris: Présence Africaine, 1964.

_____. "R.D.A., cette grande réalité." *Le Réveil*, 14 February 1949, p. 1, col. 3 and p. 3, col. 2.

_____. *Un Nègre à Paris.* Présence Africaine, 1959.

Dadié, Bernard and Terisse, André. *Les Belles histoires de Kacou Ananze, l'araignée.* Paris: F. Nathan, s.d.

Donat, Claude. "Bernard B. Dadié." *Afrique Littéraire et Artistique*, 5 (1969), 16-21.

Irele, Abiola. *The African Experience in Literature and Ideology.* London: Heinemann, 1981.

Jahn, Janheinz. *Muntu: The New African Culture.* Trans. Majorie Greene. New York: Grove Press, 1961.

Kotchy, Barthélémy. *La Critique sociale dans l'oeuvre théatrale de Bernard Dadié.* Paris: Editions L'Harmattan, 1984.

Mayes, Janis A. "Bernard Dadié and the Aesthetics of the Chronique: An Affirmation of Cultural Identity." *Présence Africaine*, 101-102 (1977), 102-118.

_____. Interviews with Bernard Dadié, January 1975, October 1978, April 1979, June 1980. Abidjan, Ivory Coast.

Mercier, R. and Battestini, S. *Bernard Dadié, écrivain ivorien.* Paris: Nathan, 1964.

Nantet, Jacques. "Bernard Binlin Dadié." *Panorama de la littérature noire d'expression française.* Paris: Fayard, 1972, pp. 69-81.

Nathan, Fernard, ed. *Bernard Dadié, écrivain ivorien.* Paris: Classiques du Monde, 1964.

Niane, Djibril Tamsir. *Sundiata: An Epic of Old Mali.* Trans. G.D. Picket. London: Longmans, 1965.

Ouologuem, Yambo. *Bound to Violence*. Trans., Ralph Manheim. New York: Harcourt, Brace and Jovanovich, 1971.

_____. *Le Devoir de violence*. Paris: Edition du Seuil, 1968.

_____. "Patron de New York." *Présence Africaine*, 53 (first trimester, 1965), 255-258.

Quillateau, Claude. *Bernard Binlin Dadié: l'homme et l'oeuvre*. Paris: Présence Africaine, 1967.

Sembene, Ousmane. *God's Bits of Wood*. Trans. Francis Prise. New York: Doubleday and Co., 1962.

_____. *Les Bouts de bois de dieu: Banty Mam Yall*. Paris: Le Livre Contemporain, 1960.

Wauthier, Claude. *The Literature and Thought of Modern Africa: A Survey*. Trans. Shirley Kay. London: Pall Mall Press, 1966.

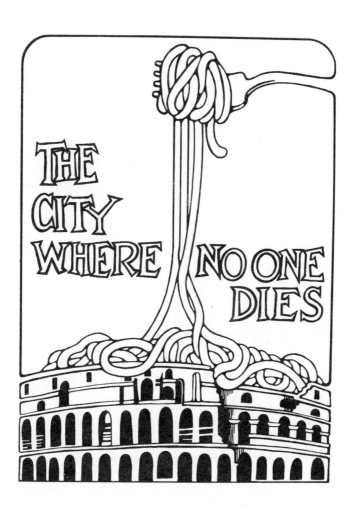

THE CITY WHERE NO ONE DIES

Can anyone in Paris contract any other disease besides fidgetitus? I've got it. Will I find a healer in this country to save me?

I'm walking, walking, walking. The boulevards, strange footpaths between the tall houses, are no longer enough for me. Footpaths swept and washed at each new dawn by booted teams of workers, civilized footpaths that divide instead of unite.

We know that you can settle along the edge of new streets without participating in their lives.

My past is struggling against the new man that I wanted to become. None of the smiles that scurry along the terraces can retain me. I need other smiles, other songs. Paris is crushing me. Paris had caressed me. Paris is biting me. And I hardly know her dark forest.

My hotel room: sonorous cage! Oh! the weight of buildings holding blinding signs on their shoulders or on their foreheads. Forest of lights, of fireflies that play at sending each other signals, at winning the attention of passersby, at retaining them for a little chat.

I'm smothering in these rectangular streets, with no capriciousness, streets drawn by heads and not by hearts, streets that are labeled, made navigable, narrow. I'm smothering in these columns of men hurriedly running away from their own work, their own shadows.

* * *

This all began one evening, at the end of a walk in the country. I had mistaken myself for a Parisian because I ran like the Parisians, because I knew how to change at Marcadet-Poissonniere or at Reuilly-Diderot, because I knew how to sip my drink through pursed lips like a baby bird. All of a sudden, I lost my balance. Paris had not digested me because I resisted. The gods from home, obstinate and patient, pulled me in another direction.

* * *

I went to take leave of my Parisian friends, just as we do at home. How do men really differ?

These Parisians who weigh their words, taint their smiles and measure their gestures, know how to shake your confidence: they make you admit that the sun rises in the West![1] Panurge no longer brings his herd to graze in Paris. So, these Parisian friends didn't stop repeating: two opposing vices, greed and luxury, shape the city, two plagues which have brought down all the great empires.

This statement was not uttered blindly. A wise man from a country named Rome had said it before, many centuries ago. This statement grew in volume, tingled in my ears, blinked in the neon signs. I heard it in the different noises of the city. The desire mounted in me to visit a country where the wisemen speak like the elders back home. In that country,[2] the old men recount their memories without being called dimwits, the wave of young graduates rocks their ears, friends are chosen according to the whims of the heart.

In that country, you don't walk with your nose to the wind ready to espouse even the unjust cause of the one who frees you from the burdensome demands of an order or a decree; nose to the wind to detect the odor of the individual who, tomorrow, will be the master of the day and under whose umbrage you will be able to lead the dreamed existence, that is to say favored, protected, feared.

Happy country where men sing the dawn without fearing the night.

Rome! magic name! vast city of quiet rhythms! If the people from here talk to you about Rome, Venice, Capri, Florence, Naples, your only resort is to leave. If a woman from here tells you: the sun! the sky! the flowers! the men; if you can imagine what she doesn't tell you; your only resort is to leave! Paris is a forest; on a street corner, a butterfly, a dragonfly, a woman and you are no longer the same.

* * *

I must go to Rome! Under her sky the offices are undoubtedly busy, the injustices less, the favors veiled. Her people, so old, are certainly made up of happy men.

I don't stop examining the flyers; a wolf suckles two children, a cathedral looks at a canoer*, immense statues, mountains overhanging lagoons, gulfs, ruins, swimming pools peopled with vacationers. I'm reading what's written about Rome because I know the Parisians' dialect a little; it's enough to hold on to the railing in this trap of perfects, imperfects in the chaos of decomposed time and in the capriciousness of moods.[3] Here, all of your intelligence, culture and finesse is contained in a certain sign called comma, the preferred sign of the Parisian.

Just to see Rome and her people rich in mummies, statues, superstitions: a people that is undoubtedly more balanced and less capricious. I must touch, with my fingers, the pedestal upon which men from here build their society, a pedestal to be compared to your own. The other aspects seem secondary to me: outgrowths caused by time, by fantasies, by whims, for the luck or misfortune of peoples. We have all let ourselves be so dazzled by the new colors of our clothes that the colors have taken precedence over clothes and men. In our time we judge each other by the glitter of our clothing, by the shape of our balconies, by the bold paintings on a canoe, by the quantity of our arrows and the number of our generals, and especially by our gold reserves. In Rome, I hope to rediscover man and not a caricature. This ancient people must have passed the stage of parades and of façades from which you look down on an anonymous, often starving and ragged crowd. Will they have realized the terrible mistake that is made throughout the world of thinking that a man on his knees, a man trembling for himself, his wife, his children, his friends, his bread, his security, is a conquered man? Will they have understood that people have spent the most productive part of their time creating bonds with one another? Will they have understood, better than others, the ties between human beings and consequently have risen above the fictive differences posted on their route like simple ordeals, simple tests? To sum it up, would I be dealing with a people who knows how to give a man an honorable place in the city?

* * *

I'm in a hurry to leave. Palm Sunday is very sad. A weak and persistent rain is falling on Paris. A civilized rain that calculates and husbands its strength, regulates its rhythm and its duration. I would like to tell the Parisians

---

*They say *gondolier* as if to differentiate themselves from us.

that I meet: at home the winds don't follow the boulevards, don't stop at traffic lights, don't slow down at crossings, at the terrace of a café. Disrespectfully, they leap over the forest, turn houses and trees upside down, plant disorder in the villages... We haven't yet muzzled the wind, bound the rain, chained the lightning, domesticated the thunder. Everything back home moves as it likes.

I don't like this tired, worn out, soft rain that seems to come from a factory or a laboratory. The city has become sad. Men huddle in cafés and under store awnings. The streets are losing their animation. Even the taxis seem to be cold.

Paris! one of our cities, misplaced along the Seine, is only beautiful under the sun!

I would like to have gone to Rome by the old pilgrims' route in order to fill myself with the importance of the city, to be permeated by all the legendary stories heard about the country, by the shape of the buildings, the color of the soil, the customs of the people with whom I would stay. Time compels me to rape the city.

I'm looking in vain for a taxi. All of them are passing without stopping, and the hands of my watch unrelentingly advance; those of a subway station clock, with their mania for jumping as if they pulled time, make me sick. What's wrong with all these Parisians? I had always thought we were the only ones to like the rain, to sing it. And suppose I changed places? Only a few steps away, a car stands empty. Just the time to go back, hop! It's gone with a passenger, almost always a woman. Ah! the Parisian women, they have a very special way of hurrying. They must have ants or live coals on their bodies since they are in such a hurry. And I'm waiting. And these hands which don't stop moving toward the hour of departure, trotting, each time pulling a little, on what I don't know, inside of me—the heart or the guts. It's cold, and I'm hot.

Finally, I jump into a radio-car almost before it has stopped, for fear that a Parisian woman will take it right from under my nose. And no more than a quarter of an hour to go from the Pantheon to the Invalides. You don't understand what a distance that is. Obviously, you don't know Paris and it's very difficult to compare the distances in Paris with the distances of another city. So don't imagine anything and just tell yourself that this distance was great, so great that the driver to whom I'm explaining my situation, nods seriously, consults his watch, spews out a few overly-friendly remarks to a taxi stopped at his side, starts off and makes a thousand detours in order to avoid the red lights and the traffic jams. But, can anyone, in Paris, avoid these two terrible maladies, which for centuries generations of specialists seem to have attacked in vain? Is it in an effort to run away from them that Parisians go so fast? Naive people! Running away from a disease that is born of agglomeration, thrives on it; a very specific disease that will die with the city! And against it, no vaccine! In this realm, the Parisian displays his impotence, but doesn't understand that salvation is found in the return to the footpaths. Obstinately, he enlarges the streets, rectifies them, numbers them, forbids passage in certain directions, imposes obligatory itineraries. A poultice on a wooden leg, as he himself expresses it so well in his self-denigration. Thus, we are twice caught in the traffic jam that endows the pedestrian with a kind of luster and wisdom. He makes a note of it, as a matter of fact, ostensibly. At the moment, everyone appears to be seated in a field of red ants. In short, leaving for Rome is decidedly not a restful enterprise.

—We'll get there, the driver mumbles, hooked to his steering wheel.

—Is it possible? Ten minutes to go.

—We have plenty of time.

—I'm telling you ten minutes.

He consults his watch, and after having exhaled his cigarette smoke, tosses off, without looking at me:

—That's even too much time.

This assurance hardly decreased my tension. On the contrary, it irritated me, because it seemed to me that Paris had used one of its terrible weapons to hold on to me and that this driver was in cahoots with his city.

Finally, the car surges into a kind of immense hall, stops in front of a door behind two other vehicles. We're there! I'm breathing so loudly that a lady takes several steps, before turning to look at me, showing me a pair of huge, frightened doe-shaped eyes. She can't understand. Not really. By the way she scrutinizes me, I realize that she has never been in a situation like mine. Ah, the inability to understand other people! Not even attempting an approach, but always and unceasingly, considering only her privileged situation. And my black head ran from this scared lady, toward the magistrates and the powerful men of the day who throw others in prison, keep them there for many years, then, finding them innocent, free them without any compensation. And I say to myself, God, see that this arbitrariness which can exist in Paris – where men, classified, categorized, differentiated, look for the cold value that they can give to each other – never reaches our shores. Because everything that has the Parisian label couldn't possibly be a universal cure-all. And wouldn't it be ridiculous to imitate Paris in her displays, her grandeur and her pettiness, in her laughter, her anger and her dreams without having understood them?

Paris doesn't judge herself according to her actions but always according to her spirit; men's actions are often in contradiction with the city's spirit, which is the epitome of hope.

In the bus that takes us away towards Orly, on the seats to the left, an old, bearded man, dressed in black. Unctuous, calculated, ponderous gestures. Undoubtedly, a man of weight, one whose name, when put in the balance, comes out to the proper, expected, required figure. His hands have the twitches characteristic of individuals who reign over thousands of consciences. They rub together, join together, cross each other, open, close. A splendid assurance emanates from his whole being. A truly happy man, confident in himself, in the future, safe from every storm, one of those upon whom it is difficult to cast any doubt. A rock. I bet that he's found the road that leads straight to paradise. An invading assurance, war-like even.

I wasn't wrong: this is a Jewish priest, excuse me, a rabbi, because here, the obsession with precision and specialization is such that the name of biped herders changes with each small tribe. This herding term could, with good cause, offend you.[4] But haven't you ever thought about mass education, about the kind of treatment meted out to those who think for themselves, haven't you ever thought about kings' fools, about the courtesans of those in power at the time, haven't you ever, from a mole-hill, watched men walk in procession or in a crowd going down the street? Now do you understand why the keepers of the peace have a kepi and a stick? For some individuals, cities are large sheep-pens, and in Paris, when the sheep has been sheared, he's no longer asked to dance, cavort, contrary to the countries where that's still required of him; countries where one has opinions; always imitating the grey lizard who, up on his front legs, looks, lowers and lifts his head again, in an ancestral, customary pose. Human lizards! Human chameleons! Supreme human perfection, finished product of the new cities! At least Paris knows how to sugar-coat the pill, as the inhabitants so maliciously express it. The fact remains that in spite of the lights and large boulevards, the herd can be hungry and cold here. For it, a truly human society is not yet within reach. Is it any more so in other places where new hungers have exasperated appetites and unleashed basic instincts?

* * *

Next to the honorable old man, a beautiful young copper-skinned girl. The color adds to her beauty, to her charm. Her black hair doesn't have the silkiness and the body of the Parisian womens' hair. Her bosom, on the other hand, is radiant! They're talking to each other. Is she his child? She's not smiling. Tense, she's looking straight ahead, seeming to relive a dream, pursuing an idea. Sometimes the corners of her mouth purse up. That's all. The old man continues to talk. A stiffened, tense young lady, who certainly hasn't had a happy youth. Marred too early, marked by a blind and pitiless society? If not, why this seriousness that is so out of place in a being made to lighten a hearth, embellish it like a flower, nurse children, caress a husband so as to chase away the worries that can darken his brow?

While looking at this Jewish girl on whose face the smile lightly glides like water off an oiled skin, I think, in spite of myself, about everything some Parisian friends have told me of the last war of extermination committed by men from this continent. War for them is almost like bowling. You play a while, you rest, and you start over again. Very curious men. They do every-thing to embellish their cities, combat diseases, augment population density, increase works of art, and then one beautiful morning, like barriers swept away, like liberated wild beasts, bitten by a past lying just below the surface, rediscovering instincts that they believed to be asleep, tamed, these men rush toward their weapons, cross frontiers and fall upon each other hysteri-cally. Almost always, those who fight, fall and die without knowing why they have died. They die upon the altar of the fatherland, for the grandeur and integrity of their country. Their country, in their eyes, is a divinity that lives upon the blood of her children. So they spend the major part of their lives forming divisions, maintaining trenches, blowing up bridges, barricading, arming themselves, frightening each other. It seems that all this stimulates sagging economies; that is, the fewer consumers there are, the more accu-mulated ruins, mutilated men, dead to be honored on prescribed days, the more men consider themselves happy. I don't know if this is just a shrewd way of making them disgusted with life. Strange conception of existence. A mass insanity that comes like an epidemic and transforms peaceful citizens, brave fathers of families, into rèal beasts. Their cities, so beautiful, so pleasant, are changed into real jungles. All means, even the most despicable, are used to bring the enemy to surrender. After having hauled out the gold, the silver, the pearls and the diamonds, they joyously kill old people, women and children. They have here, on this continent, a sovereign contempt for man. This is their weak point, and this is because in the relations that they maintain between states, between individuals, they place too much emphasis upon force. They've maintained, in spite of their immense and incontestable progress, the mentality of the ancestors of our great-great-great-grand-fathers, who armed themselves with knives, gris-gris, arrows, harpoons and, on the slightest provocation—adultery, a strip of land, fishing in waters said to be reserved—threw themselves upon each other. Our savage ancestors placed more importance upon the land than upon their own children or their fellow man. In certain areas, they hadn't attained the dazzling, dizzying progress accomplished by the Parisians and their neighbors. So the first ones could have some excuse in our eyes, but the others? How advanced and how backward at the same time! Troubling! And that makes us appreciate the education that our fathers gave us: that is, one should neither drink nor eat without thinking of his neighbor. In all circumstances, giving precedence to age. Certainly the value system based upon university degrees, which often don't make the individual, hadn't yet made its entry into our world, without ever mentioning the even more oppressive, more insolent, more degrading value system of the bank note whose existence we still ignored. Our cowry shells[5] and anklets were too heavy to transport. Today, the sumptuousness of the credit establishments crushes the houses around them. These are buildings from another class, another world. This is their time. And they are bent upon affirming it, ostentatiously, in order to avoid misunderstanding. Undoubtedly, tomorrow, man's era will come, the era of the man whom you assassinate to steal his gold, his silver, his diamonds, the man who is worth less than metals and so-called precious stones, the man who will then appreciate life because he'll no longer see it through eyes misty with tears.

While looking at this young lady, I'm thinking about all the tortures, all the atrocities committed by various people, about the degradations to which men and women have been submitted, about the burned cities, about the populations roasted like rats surprised by a bushfire in the middle of the dry season and at the time of the great wind. What pleasure can one feel, in today's world, seeing a man twisting in pain under whips, in fires, in strangleholds, hearing him give the death rattle, climbing the hill of death? Here, they just say to die. The word doesn't express forcefully enough the struggle that man puts up against death at the crucial moment, whereas to climb the hill of death gives all its importance to the tragedy. Words form us and condition our acts.[6] For the person who tortures another, dying doesn't seem to have much significance. Death here is an event that doesn't seem to affect the group as a collective body. Is this why they have so much contempt for life and for the individual? The legends, peopled with kings, queens, swords, animals, don't talk enough about man; this is perhaps why he is accorded so little importance and stirs up fire at certain periods in order to illuminate the cities. Beautiful torches, really! I'm imagining the dangers that could have been encountered by this Jewish girl who matured too early, who no longer knows how to smile, and I'm saying what a hellish world men would have if never again children knew how to sing, dance, jump, and if women, too, forgot how to smile, caress, conquer hearts.

I form one body with these two travelers who for centuries have been pursued by people of prey. Their flesh is no doubt sweet. The source of the opposition, the quarrel? A dialect, customs. A special way of imagining the world, business. A very ardent capacity in negotiation and an ardent thirst for hoarding. The God Money's most obeyed priests in his temple, the bank.

I don't even see the Ghanaian couple seated in front of me, dressed in our African way. They're going to complete agricultural training in Tel-Aviv, the Jewish capital. In this newly born state, after thousands of years of dispersion, one of the most captivating experiences for the young countries who have come upon the international scene seems to have been undertaken. The Jews, even the most erudite, apparently group themselves together in a kind of society of producers. Their first act? The lighting of a large bonfire and the throwing in of titles conquered after years and years of deprivation and struggle, to fertilize the desert with the sweat of their brow. Profound lesson! This country has not yet finished shocking the world and showing it new perspectives. Is it its daring that causes it so many tribulations? The sheepskin, as a matter of fact, doesn't grant the science of living to anyone and shouldn't give precedence to any man in a normally evolved and organized society. But how can anyone, in a world that has given primordial importance to paper and gold, love individuals who have gotten it into their heads to reverse the old order of things? Are men made for happiness? Security? If happiness were established, guaranteed, would God still have worshipers? Children who would come to him morning and evening to cry in the bosom of the church? Would land be land if there were no longer hungry, thirsty, destitute people there to make the villages, roads, and cities bloom? Society carefully maintains these contrasts, these anomalies, as if to illuminate the road passed over by those who wallow in abundance.

What distinguishes us from the Parisians? We tremble before disease, misfortune and not before God who, for us, doesn't have the terrible, fiery, spiteful face that is given to him in these countries. Our strength? We have put no limit upon the powers of the Creator. On this side of the ocean, they seem to demand of Him that he produce men of a single language, a single color, individuals having the same shape nose and same high forehead. I had to come here to understand that, in spite of their fervor, the people from these shores have a somewhat vague notion of God whom they call their Lord, a name given to their king: Lord God; My Lord the King; My Lord the bishop. God made human; men made divine. A God that is humbled; men perched out of their class. And too often, shepherds sit on the backs of skinny sheep that they have the duty to feed. Reversed roles: the sheep carry the shepherd on their frail shoulders, dress him with their fleece and feed him with their meat. And yet, that wasn't exactly the message.

Luckily, we haven't fallen into this rut because we were much closer to the Truth. Yes, we can affirm that our ancestors possessed it, this great truth. And this is exactly what gave them their great assurance in the face of all events.

Wise men, just like those from Rome; unstatued, unrecognized, unclassified, anonymous wise men, born undated, dead undated, in that way showing contempt for Time that can neither die nor grow young again; Time that doesn't count; Captive Time, condemned to follow an unending cycle, sweeping man in its rounds, in its wake. The misinterpretation of these elementary data has stamped a very special mentality on the people here. These very civilized men who have purposefully, leisurely complicated their way of life and who constantly want to play the game of high tide... Evading, submerging, uprooting everything...

The rabbi mumbles constantly. His beautiful white beard just moves up and down with a mechanical regularity. The bus is crossing Paris and all of a sudden I'm dreaming about lead-coated trains that transported human cattle dying from hunger, thirst and heat. You didn't have to be Jewish for that, but you had to place your dignity as a man in opposition to stupid orders, brutalities, extortions. It was sufficient to raise your head, a flag to proclaim your faith in another creed, to think that the ship you were on could take another course that was not the masters', to have associations and common interests, for you to be arrested, enchained, demolished. During certain periods of their history, men let themselves be led by bandits surrounded by vigilant and glutted guards. They capture a people by storm, just as you take a citadel or a boat by storm, and lay it very flat.

The old man is still mumbling, and the young lady never smiles. An unsmiling woman seems so masculine to me!

Look, a black passes, a loaf of bread under his arm. He's limping. Under the weight of what dreams is he bent like that? In the sea of whites, he seems even blacker. Perhaps this is a child of a king. Black princes could swarm in the Latin Quarter. Would they be in exile? What revolution would have driven them from their own countries?

The man buys a newspaper. What does he think about the current events that are disrupting the continents, uniting people, giving them a more critical notion of their solidarity, their unity? Does he know that people are coming back to life, emerging, that they are recovering their dignity, their voice? Does he know how these historical ghosts who are rising from the tombs are going to behave? God grant that they look neither at the chain scars on their wrists nor at those of the whip on their backs, but that they cast a lucid glance upon the time, the people, the sad human calvary and that they swear to never allow such errors to happen again.

Does he know that slowly, very slowly, with a sometimes discouraging slowness, we are turning a great page in the history of man?

He's walking, his loaf of bread under his arm. The daily bread! The pain, the affronts, the compromises!

This black has certainly joined two miseries together. But he's at home, can think of what he wants from the government, sometimes writes it down, turns up at elections without the risk of either losing his place in society or going to prison. Paris isn't fussy about such things. Doesn't he live in a country that makes only one demand: that it be recognized as still being young?[7] This old country wants you to observe children's rosy cheeks, the caresses of lovers in the squares, the smiles of old people rather than the cracks in houses. It knows that time has the rude quality of scratching men as well as their works, so that more importance is attached to what it can accomplish tomorrow than to what it has already done. With the past inventoried, classified, illuminated, placed in the forefront, held at arm's length by scholars and illustrious ambassadors, it walks calmly toward a destiny whose co-ordinates it seems to possess. So, admire the rosy cheeks of tomorrow's heroes and the smile of those who are going to pass on the torch.

* * *

The old man is still mumbling and pulling on his white beard. What stamina is involved in the banal gesture of mumbling constantly and pulling on his beard? The man who is smoking his pipe, mumbling and pulling on his beard seems like an impregnable fortress to me. What invader could conquer individuals who mumble, smile and pull on their white beards? What novelty could he bring to them? Scrap iron? They wouldn't know what to do with it. His life style? You see how old they are. His wisdom? And theirs, what would he do with it? What does he know about life, outside of the noises from the machines and what he has learned in books? Oh, but what are books, if not accounts of experiences or attempted dreams?[8] What does he know about men, apart from the screams of horror, the tears that he can make them shed, or the pretenses he can still momentarily force upon them for two sugar-coated almonds? Does he have any inkling that the teeth that smile are also ready to bite?

This calm old rabbi is a wise man.

A wise man, certainly, but what can astonish a man who undoubtedly understands the language of everything that exists on earth, just like a very old ancestor with legendary wisdom, or one of the witch doctors, certain healers at home?

How can you not be a wise man when you've been nourished by supernatural springs, when you've been positioned in relation to the world and to other creatures? But with this old rabbi, there is a very proud wisdom that exasperates, irritates, revolts. Pulling on his beard! Constantly mumbling while smiling and watching the people jostling about! What soldier, what new master can stand such a placid and mocking stare? Can anyone, even with submachine gunfire, bring such an individual to change his ways?

Hasn't this man given the supreme gift of a God to the world? What else does anyone want from him? His gold? If he gave up God the Son, it was in order to better guard his gold. Couldn't anyone, after making such a sacrifice, pull on his beard in all tranquillity and watch men fidget? Might the gift be poisoned? Has the power of gold eclipsed that of God? Would anyone want to build society upon other bases? Accord man more liberty, freedom, peace? Just so many more insolvable questions for the black observer that I am who understands poorly why the people here feel a seasonal, periodic itching, like a volcanic eruption, to set out after another category of men in order to settle, as they say, a very old quarrel that should have been buried centuries ago.

* * *

—Anything to declare?

I perk up my ears, turning my head like a rooster!

—Anything to declare?

—Nothing, I say, raising my arms instinctively.

—Do you have any money on you?

Ah, what a country! Always questions, about you, about the reason for your journey, about your friends, old diseases you've had, and what have you. A people of strange breeding.

—Any money?

—Yes, I said money, replied the customs agent, impatiently.

His ears, cheeks, and nose got red. His eyes grew round. Ho! the veins on his neck are getting blue, trying to rise out of the depths where they are embedded.

What a ridiculous question. Who goes to a foreign country without taking a little money? Any money on me? What a stupid, insensitive, even impolite question. Asking a traveler if he has any money on him, well, that's insulting to him, that's treating him like a vagabond, a liar, almost like a thief and bringing upon yourself the forces of our justice from home. For someone to ask his wife, his child, and, if worse comes to worst, a friend if he has any money is conceivable, but asking a stranger this question is the epitome of bad breeding. Here, that seems normal, so normal that some faces light up in astonishment when I take some time to respond. Bah! they have their practices and their laws. And now the customs officer's ears are getting redder. They even seem to be moving, shifting. The veins in his neck are getting fuller under his stretched skin. It seems that these are the first signs of a violent rage. This is hardly the time to take on a whole brigade of men and papers. Then too, the scandal of having people point their fingers at me must be avoided at any expense. A stranger, an outsider; our old wisdom, together with my interlocutor's flaming ears, dictate my answer:

—Yes, I say, crossing my arms.

I thought that I was through, but no, alas! The man looks at me and finally realizes that I am not a Parisian. I breathe more easily. Wrong! Raising his head suddenly, he says to me:

—How much?

What! What! Am I in a civilized country? What sick curiosity. Obligating me to say in public what I possess monetarily amounts to undressing me. That's it! Yes! the customs officer doesn't understand, being glued to his papers, that he's violating my dignity. What strange customs! Naked, in front of these women, men and children! Why does anyone hide his money so carefully? Isn't it so that he can deceive others? Ah! Until just then, I had thought that the Parisian was a very civilized, well-bred man, respecting the manners and customs of other people. And here's a customs station waking me up, opening my eyes! Evidently, because I don't have the capacity to get red, my customs officer doesn't understand that his indiscreet questions make me uncomfortable and angry. If only I could get red, red in my ears, face, hands, I could make the impatient lady to my right understand that I am not indifferent to her, make this customs officer understand that I don't see things the way he does. He doesn't even notice that my nostrils are heaving with anger, swelling as if to take away all his air and cut off his breath. How happy the chameleon must be to be able to change colors as he pleases! But can you be a chameleon at will, without having a little chameleon blood? And I have blood ill-suited for any mutation. Since the laws permit no stretching, I had to suffer under their power. So looking my customs officer in the eyes, I tell him as if to flatten him under the weight of my fortune:

—Fifty thousand francs.

Solid like the law, and scornful at the same time:

—You are allowed only twenty thousand francs!

—What? Twenty thousand for Rome, Naples, Florence, Capri, Genoa, Milan?

I strang out the names to make an effect, to create compassion around me, to soften the attitude of my interlocutor, distract him a moment and...he remained inflexible. He had already seen so many men like me pass, had put his hand in so many suitcases that had gone around the entire world, that he looks at me calmly this time and repeats with firmness, a firmness that means, let's stop the dialogue:

—You are only allowed twenty thousand francs.

Hum! Rome must certainly be either a dangerous rival or a small village for Paris to have so little regard for her. Twenty thousand francs! It would be better to go back to my country. Ah! if only I could call off this trip so teeming with adventures! What dignity do I have left to save, now that everyone knows that I have fifty thousand francs to my name.

—Twenty thousand francs, I say arrogantly, to show that at home we would have had more regard for someone who naively confessed to having money on him. Sincerity has a charm about it that disarms the most intransigent judges.

—Yes, sir, twenty thousand francs; that's the rule. Next! The customs officer brought me back to reality. There was a line stretching behind me, an impatient line of travelers wondering why people as obstinate as I wanted to travel without knowing anything about the customs practices. I stood there, looking at him, pretending to think, not knowing what to do next to make myself understood. Out of arguments and breath.

—If you want anything else, go to the chief. Hey! they have chiefs here, just like back home! He should have said that earlier! Such organization and they don't even understand that they shouldn't humiliate travelers the way they have me! Someone will be able to show me some justice. With chiefs, we are always understood because we know how to judge their mood of the moment, we know how to surround them and tell them what they want to hear. Praises make them sprout wings, stumble, and...sometimes lose their bearings. Ah! how slow a customs officer is to indicate the right path! A chief! nothing in the world is easier to exploit; examples abound of those who make a living on chiefs by carrying their photographs around, by selling their photographs, by singing their praises, going so far as to call them God's chosen ones! And these men succeed in convincing themselves that they are actually new Messiahs, but Messiahs now inextricably associated with breweries, banks, sanitation services, hearses, gas stations, shipping; Messiahs who have chosen the earth for Paradise and who crowd the merchants into a temple whose veil will no longer be torn up. The cross? They've generously abandoned it to the people. Theirs is a very small one in gold. Christ's example hasn't been highly contagious. Quite to the contrary: they've learned their lesson from it. And they intend to be saved by men that they cannot save. The only agreed upon sacrifice is to talk constantly about sacrifice, and then they hold out the hat to be filled. The new tax! in countries where men rarely think about what they're doing and consequently give without counting! Loyal partners building an anachronistic world filled with storms and floods...Is it with one of these many chiefs that I'm going to do business? Composing myself, I enter an office where four men dressed in black are working.

—The chief, please.

—The chief? asks one of the men.

—Yes.

—What do you want with him?

Here it is, the protective wall around the chief.

—What do you want with him?

—I would like to speak with him.

There he is, the employer tells me, pointing with the tip of his ink pen to the man who hadn't raised his head either upon my arrival or during the discussion. They're all alike, these chiefs, they need a servant. The chief who is pointed out with the tip of an ink pen undoubtedly doesn't have the respect of all of his subjects, unless in this country, men of his importance refuse to be pointed out with a finger. I've heard that pointing at someone with a finger could bring many misfortunes upon him. Is it to ward off destiny then that the chief is pointed out with the tip of a pen?

Bald. He must have clear, luminous ideas, with such a shiny skull; an admirable skull, gone over with sand paper.

Upon seeing this superb skull, I say to myself: the Parisian woman will be truly equal to the man when she agrees to walk down the boulevards with such a highly polished skull, this veritable mirror upon which files, dossiers, the ventilator were reflected. Ah! these Parisian subjects must not be easy to rule.

Anyway, the chief raises his head, scratches the small bunch of hair hooked to his ears, as if to beg me to let him keep it as a souvenir, not to create any new worries for him. Who could be insensitive to such a request? This skull, this border of hair hidden behind the ears, and then, even more, this soft, benevolent look!

How can I present my request so that these last vestiges remain? Ah! you're laughing, my friend. Hair that falls out is like a tooth that is lost, it disfigures you...

* * *

I don't know what men think about the brigadiers in Parisian airports, but for me, they're the great guys, model, up-to-date chiefs, open to all ideas, exceptional beings who understand in a few minutes all the situations in which a passenger could find himself. I began to think that hair in abundance could be an obstacle in the exchange of ideas, just like the "functional" Parisian homes—"nests" serving as a barrier to the effusion of hearts. Don't go deducing from that, primo, secondo...tertio, no! nothing... Why would anyone travel if it wasn't to compare, to reason and to attempt to look for that which brings us together with others? A gesture still practiced in one country is undoubtedly a gesture forgotten somewhere else. Excavations must be done throughout the world, because time, without our realizing it, deposits on man the sediments that color or discolor him, that atrophy or develop him beyond measure.

So I'll explain to the chief that, having come from Africa to Paris, I was on the verge of going back, but some kinsmen or some compatriots had spoken to me so highly about Rome that I couldn't resist the desire to see this city; that I had to prove to my people that I had really just come from Rome by bringing them small souvenirs, and after leaving Rome, prove to the children from the *concession*⁹ I would go back to, that I really am African by passing out a little money among them as is the practice back home. In order to fulfill these two imperatives, his country's laws would only allow me the petty sum of twenty thousand measly francs! The chief-brigadier, with the intuition that a true customs officer has for feeling and grasping everything, understood that I had unfortunately placed the honor of an entire country upon my fragile shoulders, just as the honor of an entire corporation of vigilant agents was weighing upon his. He touched two or three books, looked for some idea on the table as he ran his fingers over it, glossed over his forehead as if making the last feathers fall from it; all of a sudden his forehead lit up, and raising his nose toward the sky, calling it to witness the purity of his intentions, and, for me, who must have been having lucky days, stretched the rules slightly and allowed me ten thousand more francs.

Praise be forever to the African Gods who constantly come to our aid in these countries where everything seems to be done to disorient, disarm us. I nearly danced! Euh! ten thousand francs, it gives you wings, makes you dizzy! After all that! everyone knows that I have thirty thousand francs for traveling expenses. Consequently, my life style is known, calculated! If ever I exceeded my allotment, they would try to find out where the extra money came from, and I would be classed among the people that could be suspected. What a strange country where the inhabitants live exposed while believing themselves to be safe behind the walls of houses! Naked men, that time hasn't dressed very well yet. They can talk to me about coats, jackets, smoking jackets, full-length coats that we'll probably adopt one day through pure exoticism; does that prove that all of them are dressed? Well dressed?...

These men, with their sometimes cramped gestures, have organized their existence in such a way that our life is more intimate behind the bamboo fixings of our undecorated straw houses, behind our dried clay walls with no gilt ceilings.

Our contempt for gold has undoubtedly saved us from dangerous tropisms. To us, the eyes of our fellow men don't yet appear as escarbuncles, diamonds or other precious stones to be pulled out, and their sweat as fertile manure for sterile lands, or first choice oil for rusty machines. In this regard, we can still be placed in the flattering category of a young people. A youth that will pass quickly if ever one day we enter into contact with the people from here; and it is even to be feared that we'll beat them in the rush for gold, trampling everything underfoot, including our own children.

I don't pretend that we don't look in on our neighbors from time to time to get food for conversation, but it's done with discretion, out of the corner of one's eye, as we say – pretending to see nothing, to hear nothing, and yet recording everything...Here, individuals station themselves boldly right in the middle of the road, in the center of the compound to show that they're seeing you, observing you, lighting you up with the fire from their eyes, for if they looked through shutters, a very important detail, a tic that would be valuable for their investigations, could escape them. It's in public and not in private that you're asked questions about your position, about your wealth, your acquaintances, about everything that you hold strictly private. It has even become very dangerous to walk down violently lit avenues and boulevards at certain hours of the night: death through the weapon of a hungry person is lying in wait for you; back home, the most you can expect is to meet up with a genie who won't even always be bad. In an effort to gather the information that you might have failed to give, they'll send a thick cloud of domesticated and well-trained flies after you. The malicious Parisian guarantees that our countries will be overpopulated with them very soon. What fly could he be referring to? Well, once again, it is proven that people from these countries recognize their kinship with insects and animals. They even have a science with a complicated name that is devoted to tracing in man the instincts of the cow, the ass, the sheep, the hog, the rabbit, the wolf, the calf, the lion, the fox, the eagle, the vulture, the snake, the chameleon, and what else, I don't know. They join us together in some hasty round-about way, like men trying to find themselves. So, I remain convinced that we'll end up by helping each other when we have the same conception of its role in society. So the fly is a new kind of human creature that comes, talks with you, and then, with its stomach very fat with news, flies off to empty itself to those who pay him for his harvest...

Thirty thousand francs...What can I do with thirty thousand francs in a place like Rome, that everyone talks about with feeling? However, I considered myself richer than all the other travelers, believing, naively, that they only brought in twenty thousand francs. Smiling, they looked at me. I had complacently shown my innocence, demonstrated my lack of understanding of underground laws, the paths beyond the rules. As for them, they knew the ropes!...Hush...

What's remarkable in these countries over here is the persistence with which the laws are evaded. Even before a law has seen the light of day, trenches have already been dug that will pass around it. Moles! Now I understand the meaning of corridors, passageways, cellars and levels.

A woman's voice cries out: Air France passengers for Rome, Tel-Aviv, to the boarding gate. In the voyages to the unknown, women make the announcement. Voices of sirens. A clever Parisian trick to charm the traveler and dissipate his apprehensions.

In Indian file, we enter a room where a worker invites us to wait. The room where Paris, one last time, tries to retain you with her flowers, her perfumes, her books, her sugar-coated almonds, her women with batting eyelashes enhanced by black mascara. You can still get the forgotten gift, completely empty your pockets, give back to Paris the bank note she covets so much. The stalking saleswomen observe you, lie smilingly in wait for you with a real commercial insistence. A permanent smile, sweet voices and what consideration...Against those who are leaving, whether happy or discontented, they constitute Paris' rear guard.

How indifferently you can leave a city where nothing is holding you back! By dint of roaming around the world, tearing yourself apart at each departure, you end up by no longer having attachments anywhere. You leave like an automaton, like a person who has no family; you embark without being seen off, and you arrive without being met.

That's my solution as I take the plane.

The rabbi is seated next to me. A silent neighbor. We're flying over the Parisian suburbs. A waiter, which the international language, paving the way for tomorrow's unity, calls a steward, offers us newspapers and magazines. On the first page of the magazine that I have taken, a colored map of France, with regions undoubtedly equal in terms of the favors that the government gives them. I don't think that the Dijonnais has the advantage over the Marseillais or that a president, because he came from Normandy, would only assist that corner of the land and its inhabitants. The regionalism here wouldn't be exacerbated like it could be in certain countries where thurifers spend their time favoring one tribe at the expense of the others. Every passenger has his nose plunged in a book or a newspaper.

You have to come to Paris to grasp how dramatic is the future of countries who despise writers and put them on the index. Can the rush to make a quick personal fortune explain this behavior? Could the countries that have an hysterical need for might in order to grow and affirm themselves enter into the concert of Europe exhibiting no other claim but gold reserves? The states that run after the tons of gold aren't far from transforming their assemblies into figurehead bodies where only the president has the right to speak, with a strong, well-fed court, trained to sing his praises, surrounding him. Writers, I'm no longer unaware of it, are a dangerous group, knowing how to hold neither tongue nor pen, but what human group doesn't have its heralds. Ah! how I would like to shout to all those in the world who are trying to transform people into pigs...give dreamers a chance! Give creators a chance! It's thanks to them that you will gain a taste for life. They embellish it for you for a crust of bread.

The voice of a singer who revives hope, a stanza of poetry, a passage from a book that detains a being on the verge of suicide, are more necessary than all the riches piled up, heaped up, or shown off in sumptuous salons. What kind of existence would we have if we had to spend our time listening to political speeches? Give dreamers a chance! Give the word a chance! Give the sun a chance!

Why these reflections? How many things can go through your mind when you're traveling by plane! Here, ideas are free; no boundary, no policeman to stop them. They frolic and stick to everyone's hair, as if underlining the equality of man and affirming even more the inanity of colors.

The old man is still mumbling.

Suddenly, from out of the blue, an old story told by a Parisian friend comes back to me.[10] There was, he said, in the tropics, a country where everything went very well. Briskly, the people walked in step. Starved, overexploited, they walked nonetheless, without ever asking questions or, at least, without ever raising the tone of their voices. The entire world press sang the praises of this disciplined country, ordered in its misery. One might have thought that the young men, upon their return from their trips around the world, with the unselfishness that distinguishes them, the thirst for justice that is one of their attributes, would have allowed themselves to throw back the leaden cloak that smothered their forebears. Alas!...they were the very first to scramble for spoils, to go back to the old days. Agile, they elbowed each other violently to be in the forefront so that nothing could escape them. Men who were aware had the painful feeling of finding themselves in a drifting boat. But the journalists, generally shrewd, caught up in who knows what whirlwind or what spell, no longer concerned themselves with anything but the splendor of buildings, the opulence of forms, the glimmer of state receptions, with forced smiles and the official doctrine of optimism. New Gods had taken the place of old ones, or, more exactly, had identified with them in order to exploit the riches of the country. A marriage of reason and interest at the same time, and so carefree that the people didn't stop dancing to feed their misery or escape their hunger...

I understood how lucky we were to have so different a country, wisely guided by velvet hands that never appear to get rusty, a country in which new Gods don't multiply by a strange phenomenon of schizogenesis and whose leaders, very worried about our future, spend their nights pondering what must be done for the sole happiness of our people. A country where business is growing at top speed, where injustices are unknown, factions abolished, and fawning suppressed. A small paradise where only men of authentic value can be called upon to serve their people. So the elite is composed of men from all social levels without the stupid requirement of diplomas, which are accepted begrudgingly because those who are directing our destiny know that it can be to their advantage to appoint relatives with no qualifications to certain top positions.

A plane has just passed, like an arrow. As if it had indicated the time to the rabbi, he takes some cookies out of a bag and eats them. Then he drinks from a silver goblet, wipes his mouth with the back of his hand, puts the goblet and the remaining cookies away, and starts to pull his beard again. He didn't even ask me to share his meal. A serious infraction of our rules of courtesy. What difference is there between this man next to me and myself? He's Jewish, and I'm African; he's a rabbi, and I'm Roman Catholic. I'm the brother of the Messiah that he gave up to the world. Is that why he didn't ask me to share his meal? Did he know it? Had he read this in my behavior? What more does he owe me after having given me a God? He pulls his beard and casts a proud glance over the travelers.

Descendant of Abraham, Jacob, David, Moses, Solomon, he comes from a long and glorious past: hence his self-confidence. He knows what he has been, what he is, what he owes the men who persecute him. They can ruin him, chase him, kill him. They cannot destroy his contribution to the history of humanity.

Since early childhood, I have lived as a satellite of Rome, which gives a special character to each one of my acts. Next to this rabbi with confident gestures, I now ask myself whether the African Gods have taken on Roman dress and begun to speak Latin, whether a gulf has not been created between them and me.

Disciple of the one who multiplied bread and fish and distributed them freely to the people, I have been living for the past few years in a society where men who work themselves to death hardly succeed in making ends meet. Individualism, frantic selfishness, have frightened me throughout my travels. Men who don't even look at each other, neighbors who hardly speak to each other! Cities exist where individuals die from hunger and cold, where neighbors can die and lie undiscovered for months in their room; if by chance in Rome, city of charity, seat of Christianity, of a fraternity that is a bit harassed throughout the world by the monstrous designs of different groups, there were people going around in rags, with empty stomachs, scrounging through trash cans and sleeping under bridges, one would have to admit that the world on this side of the ocean is very sick. Christianity having failed in its mission would have to be redesigned on a human scale, that is, brought back to its first principles and not allowed to be a mere emblem on the doorstep of a civilization that has the most absolute contempt for the individual. God let it be otherwise, because how would I look to my people, I who have always spent my time denigrating their Gods and their practices.

The airline stewardess comes back to speak to me in English. I answer her in her language. She smiles while whispering:

— I thought you were American.

— I'm a black American who's learning to speak French.

— You speak it marvelously.

I sprouted wings; I started to fill up my seat. Ah, men! how little it takes to daze them, intoxicate them, to make them lose perspective. My wings are touching the ceiling of the plane. Fortunately, they're invisible.

Parisians are not difficult, when I consider that in certain countries, you could find men who would categorize us, you and me, as young school children because we didn't have a certain diploma to which the Parisian wouldn't even attach a value anymore. This lack of a diploma would have been a serious handicap all our lives. When considering inviting us to certain receptions, someone would say: They don't have the "bac."[11] If we tried to play a worthwhile role in the concert of work forces at the construction yard that a new country represents, someone would sing: They don't have the bac. If we wanted to be paid a decent salary, someone would shout: They don't have the bac!

At every crossroad, someone would have demanded that we exhibit the head of a high school graduate, a B.A. stomach, an M.A. heart, and I don't know what kind of feet! Ah! if we could only open up every man's stomach, measure the intestines, we would actually realize that they are the same color, the same length, and that the time spent on school benches, often at the expense of the working masses, doesn't add one additional centimeter to the organ.

Luckily, Paris is a city where the spirit can flourish; if not, there wouldn't be enough prisons in which to confine men. How many countries would profit by walking toward this point in the furrows of this spiritual city. How you would like to shout to certain men that circumstances have brought to power: Hail, Caesar! Those who are dying from fatigue, from cold, from hunger and from injustice, greet you!

One hour of traveling and how many ideas have attacked me, beseiged me! How they should be pitied, the pilgrims of earlier times, who went to Rome on foot. It's not surprising that most of them became saints. In scrapping for months on end with certain more or less ridiculous ideas, faith is purified, fortified, proliferates and sometimes becomes all-invading and intransigent. Everything is brought back to oneself, to one's very small light, to the scrap of acquired truth. Whereas Truth is the sum of truths. Anxious to have a first-rate place in the sky, to possess the largest crown, they think they are serving the Creator, putting themselves in his good graces, becoming his most docile sons, the most cherished, by blowing out brains and scattering intestines. How many men have believed they were guaranteeing their salvation by accumulating bones at the feet of a God of love and of mercy! If you examined certain halos closely, you would not only find blood spots, borders of blood, but also a few bits of tibia. No! no one serves God by immolating his creatures to him.

And how many men we kill in a thousand ways and under thousands of circumstances!

In the West, you can have a peaceful conscience, because it suffices to be pardoned by a priest for God to forgive the crime committed. A perfectly well-organized world that accords everyone complete peace of mind. God is only severe for those whom his interpreters condemn, and he has no intention of disagreeing with the latter, it seems, for fear that certain errors might not continue to flourish and foster our blindness and our faith.

My neighbor finally breaks his silence.

— You speak English?

I proffer my right ear, smiling like a deaf mute.

— You speak English?

I shake my head. An international language like crying, smiling, dancing, hugging, dreaming...

—I'm sorry.

He's sorry that I can't speak the most widely accepted language in the world, the only cultured language because it's used by a strong, rich, powerful, disciplined, respected and feared people. A people, intrepid and conscious of its rights, its value, its riches.

—I'm sorry!

A language having proved itself on every continent and having converted thousands to its use...he takes out his passport to fill out the embarkation card. A naturalized American, he was born in Hungary. Through his gestures he makes me understand that such petty formalities don't exist in his adopted country, which is a gigantic land where freedom flourishes. In his land, where Liberty, statuefied, mummified, welcomes you waving a huge torch that blinds the people, while permitting a minority to see their interests more clearly, each person can live as he likes and think as he likes as well...as long as his form of thinking isn't contrary to the admissable norms and to the forms of thinking laid down and guaranteed by the Constitution. There, blacks no longer live on the fringes of society, according to him, even though their complexion could still frighten some uninformed men. If some of them rot on the city's doorstep, it's because they won't accept doing what everyone else does: exhibiting the light coloring demanded in the guise of an identity card. Besides, you have to admit these blacks aren't really making any effort to bleach themselves, to Americanize themselves, when you think that after several centuries of contact, the great majority still maintain their original color. Undigested men that years and bad weather have left unaltered. As for the whites, each year they become whiter, in his view, so that the flame of liberty will rise higher in a sky invaded by young democracies with iron fists and class structures carefully maintained in the best interests of civilization.

Still through gestures, he asks me to visit this new paradise for which he shows me a prospectus. This Garden of Eden is divided into two parts, the North and the South. The latter, a monolithic unity, strangely resembles a puzzle; the North, on the contrary, has more imagination in its contours, thus is certainly more open in spirit. Isn't a people the reflection of its continent, another product of the land? A country that has lakes, islands, bays, is an "expansive," imaginative, spiritual country; the inhabitants submit to influences other than granite, marble or sand and that makes them men of a certain vision, of particular ideas.

The old States, anxious to preserve their values, to contain the barbarians of the century, have a morbid taste for formalities. They are like old people who surround themselves with medications against rheumatism and other diseases that daily lie in wait for them. You must, at every moment, at every turn, give proof of having spent time in school, by the sheer quantity of the forms you are required to fill out. Luckily, schooling is obligatory. But wouldn't this be a clever way of training and developing people's memories, because the same information is almost always required.

At first, I was ashamed to admit each time that I didn't know how to read or write. I shocked my interlocutors by swearing not to know the date of my arrival into the world. It wasn't really a capital event for me. To mock time, to disappear without leaving any trace, without even saying good-bye to friends and relatives, seemed monstrous. And yet this is just how we live, how we treat time, how we act in this ocean of air in which we move. From the ocean of air to the tumulus of earth, there is no gap.[12] In the West, on the

58

contrary, you must count, calculate, mark everything to prove to time that you exist and that you expect some consideration.

Not to know your age is really to participate in eternity and to see yourself as an integral part of the universe. After all, who really knows his age? From the African point of view, that's understood. Now, is this way of viewing man in the world false? Being born, playing a bit of a role and going away!...

—Lake Geneva! the captain shouts to us.

A very reputable lake where rich men come to get fresh air and statesmen take a rest from their many fatigues. How much of its majesty a mountain loses when you fly over it! These white summits that I would have peopled with genies before whom I would have trembled with fear, ready to deprive me of everything I possess in return for their favors, these mountains, humbly, march past beneath me. Undoubtedly, the men how live at the foot of these tormented peaks suffer from their caprices and attribute such to capricious demons. Just the fact of flying over these summits, of contemplating them from above, instills indefinable powers in me. I feel like a new man, a strong, powerful man, different[13] from those who throw themselves at the feet of these giants, giants for them because seen from below. After such observations, why be astonished that certain individuals, risen above the ranks, should feel some contempt for the seething mass at their feet? That beings, from whom one can get favors, in the long run, should take themselves for small gods to be honored morning and evening? I'm dominating these gigantic mountains caressed by white clouds, these mountains that seem to be sleeping under their shroud; and yet it would take so little for the plane, which distorts my perspective on things, to break into pieces and restore the real dimensions to everything. I'm contemplating. Our proverb is right in saying, "It's good to rise up, but while always looking behind you."

Jagged slopes and villages similar to the locks of hair on a woman's head. A country without a forest where no monkeys leap about, where no palm rats come and go, where no bird sings, is it a country of good spirits, in the sense that we speak of back home?

Was Rome conquered? By whom? At the time of the conquest, did traitors betray patriots as is the practice today? Were steles raised against those men? Did their descendants, with time and forgetfulness, end up adopting the cloak of the super patriot? Is Rome going to offer me the spectacle of the same errors, the same dead weights that are inherited and dragged on, the same injustices that are maintained and cultivated in certain other lands? The same misappropriation of funds by public officials?

In Rome, is a man's worth measured by the number of offices he holds, by the advantages he has accumulated, by the length of his car, by the price of the suit that he wears?

Is his worth dependent upon the importance of his court? the number

59

of his wives? And especially, especially upon his ability to reverse his position? Cleverness they say! Isn't this cleverness the most obvious sign that society, in its present form, which requires the use of several masks, hasn't yet been suited to man? Aren't we making our human communities into types of forests, jungles where more distrust is cultivated?

Ah! undoubtedly I'm expecting too much from vaunted Rome, from Rome which seems to be the cradle of the sumptuous civilization that I saw blossom in Paris. I have a strong impression of going back to a source to see if the water upstream is different in color from that below. In other words, has this civilization that came from Rome taken on a local color in Paris? What difficulties were experienced by the Parisians in adapting themselves to new forms of life?

Banal questions! I ask them, however.

"Elba Island!" whispers the microphone. Here, a great Parisian general who prevented the continent from sleeping was forced to reside. Having taken himself for a dressmaker, he took extreme pleasure in cutting out kingdoms. Europe's appearance not pleasing him, he was intent on giving it a more agreeable, more smiling physiognomy, and to that end spent the best part of his days taking bridges, capitals, propagating terror, burning cities. It had become so commonplace to destroy cities that certain of them, at the approach of this thunderous warrior, set themselves on fire so as to be a part of his followers, to illuminate his march, mark his routes, immortalize themselves by entering into his glorious future legend. Very intelligent cities which today have their names engraved in the marble of Paris' largest war monument. At any rate, this man, having succeeded in escaping from the island, regained power and called himself Napoleon. I thought that only men from home changed names when changing conditions. How we all resemble each other, though separated by millions of kilometers! This general, who became emperor, didn't always recognize those who helped him to rise to the height of power. A specific disease of great people who very often prefer to surround themselves only with colorless men who mirror their grandeur, courtesans, and at their feet, carpets of no importance.

Captured during the course of one of the greatest battles of this continent's history, this terrible emperor was again sent to an island. Did his enemies want to make him understand, in this way, that you can be great and at the same time know how to humble yourself, that you have to know how to be great when you reign over men like yourself? and that you are truly great only in so far as you seek the happiness of those you command? As restless as he might be, an island was still immense for an emperor alone with himself. No head of state should ever forget the lesson of obligatory confinement to an island.

The people here like to speak through symbols, even citing proverbs and throwing in their own anecdotes, which make them laugh until they cry.

They don't laugh all the time, but, once they start, they do as well as us. If in the city they are afraid to make some trinket fall, in the country no restraint is imposed upon laughing. They even tease each other when they're from different regions, just like we Abrons and Essoumas laugh at each other...[14]

Alive, this emperor had many enemies. Dead, his ashes are still fought over! Majestic ashes. Exactly like back home where the ashes are of more value than the living man.

How naive the Europeans of the time were to think that a general accustomed to great marches on horseback could live on a tormented, arid island, with no court, bugle, banner!

Does the boat still exist that the general took to flee Elba Island? The Parisians must have put it in some museum. The rewarding mania for conserving everything, for taking inventory, classifying, labeling everything, which allows a people to measure the road traveled to situate itself in time, to prove with supporting evidence, and sometimes to deceive itself with an apparent good faith!

* * *

Here we are in Rome's sky, which all of a sudden surrenders itself in all its expanse. Penetrating a city by air constitutes a tragic violation. All of its defenses are torn down. Here, there, new buildings with yellow roofs. The rabbi doesn't stop mumbling. For millions of years, with patience, the same patience he uses to mumble and pull his beard, he's been waiting with his people for the Savior announced by the prophets. The one who reigns in Rome and whom Rome has assumed the duty of making known throughout the world, is not his. Rome for him is not in any way a holy city, a metropolis.

He raises his head, straightens his glasses, puts away his book. The beautiful Jewish woman with a complexion verging on gold and copper comes close to me in order to see the city through the porthole. Two gold teeth, a child's gentle eyes and a baby's delicate smile. While looking at her, I think about the war in spite of myself. When the animal in man has risen up, must he at all times and all places, hang his head?

In the name of what and why do people still make war? Is it to show that, as authentic descendants of old warriors, they don't intend to abandon any of their ancestral practices? It's an extreme pleasure for them to destroy the nettles in the Celestine fields; and the nettles are the men who have another color, another language, other customs. Often it's your neighbor. The white man's god doesn't have the right to produce different types. A mold is imposed on him. And everything that is created of this mold is the work of the devil whom men have decided to combat on all fronts. These people intend to impregnate and not to be impregnated. Taking themselves for the males of the world, they seem to have a very narrow vision of the universe. Is it from selfishness, from fear of renewal? This living, teeming, spirited world, being transformed from day to day, is frozen for them. They no longer know how to make room for a neighbor because they no longer have real, close ties with what surrounds them. Everyone here is placed on a pedestal from where he looks at other creatures. And because he is on his pedestal, he wants the others to pay him homage.

And all this inspires their morbid taste for burning cities that took millions of years to build, shedding blood, throwing children full of life into the flames. From this point of view, they are still very primitive.

And I suspect that in these rigorously cold countries, they love fire to the point of making it into an exacting god. Do they think that after its passage, their purified cities and fields will be better sanctuaries? However, the country is so beautiful and the inhabitants have, through their ingenuity, their industriousness, enhanced their existence with a thousand little nothings that make life charming. The streams, the mountains, the grass, the flowers, the birds, everything combines to catch the attention of the foreigner.

These things are like the pepper in our sauces. They season the character of cities and countries and make life here very elating. But could this pepper go to their heads at certain times of the year and release the destructive madness in them? They seem to be persuaded that men would never think about God, would never allow themselves to be exploited, if they always had dry eyes and didn't work continuously for a peace rendered elusive by their myriad machinations. For peace is just as highly appreciated here as it is with us. It is in order to assure it, affirm it, establish it, that they spend the major part of their lives making war on each other.

They are truly incomprehensible people who carry the cross in one hand and a rifle in the other. Either you bow your head, or it is blown off! No alternative.

The specialty of the day is cold war. All the newspapers serve it to their clients. In these countries they live in anticipation of a coming war, imminent, prepared for day by day and against which the people can do nothing. They accept it, submit to it, are eaten up by it. The speeches of the heads of State are constant threats: "Don't go beyond the river which serves as our border." "Don't make overtures to my people." "If you attempt to aid certain countries within my sphere of influence, the peace is broken." "If you sell your products in a certain region, I will declare war on you."

A terribly sick taste for isolation, possession. A diabolical obsession with ruling, dominating, limiting man in his possibilities, keeping him in chains. Sheep or dogs, that is the lot of the masses. Isn't it a criminal act to denature man through hunger and fear?

Do the Europeans understand the lesson of a plane trip? Before it would have taken months and months to cover the distance now traveled in less than two hours. Has the airplane put an end to kilometers, frontiers? Why have old boundaries remained rooted in the soul, the hearts of men? A sense of ownership. This is our water! This strip of land, this mountain is ours!...Opposing the North to the South, the East to the West! Interest groups...for which one must die in order to safeguard privileges. And these wars, these fraternal struggles will be waged in the name of God, Right, Liberty. Each soldier finds in this gamut a legitimate reason to joyously sacrifice his life. And they will save the threatened fatherland by working to enrich certain families. Blood, in Europe, is profitable for a certain class of butchers. Men are still considered cattle that can be slaughtered to augment the revenues of a certain society. Will Rome speak to me in a more reassuring, more human language?

My eyes fall upon the Jewish girl who's speaking American. She has a velvet gaze, a way of looking at you altogether different from that of the airline stewardess. And I say to myself: "Some men come to blows by discussing these two different looks." Entire groups of men, who understand nothing about life, want to bend it to their whims, to their ideas, so that it will correspond to their own established position. What we want is to bring the others to us, and not to go to them, or to understand them. Therein lies the whole problem of our society.

Oh! how many exploited people spend their time applauding those who forge chains!

The old rabbi is a wise man. His serenity wins me over and I admire him. He's certainly no longer waiting for a Messiah to come to save men, but for men who can mutually esteem and save each other. He has a rough task when you think that warriors smoke out men in the temples, burn down and tarnish churches, dynamite mosques, go to battle after having eaten the flesh of Jesus Christ, heard a sermon about charity and brotherhood. This preparation helps them to better defeat the enemy, the barbarian, the foreigner; the unfortunate brother from the other camp. The poor are encouraged to earn heaven before they earn the earth. And they fall into the trap. Through patriotism.

He doesn't want to have dealings with robots, the old rabbi, but with men in the real sense of the term. He knows the sad history of his people. Even if he had adopted Jesus Christ, the strong nations would have taken him away by force. For them, everything is conquered, even a god.

That being the case, what good would it do to pull chestnuts out of the fire for others? Why be saddled with a useless burden? No one can deny that Jesus comes from his tribe. They can't speak of him without mentioning Jerusalem, Bethlehem, Nazareth, without evoking all of Israel's history. But if his ancestors had adopted Jesus, would those people have accepted with the same complacency, the same love, to be bombarded with the genealogy of the Judges, the psalms of David, the proverbs of Solomon? Wouldn't they have screamed scandal, chauvinism? Today, there they are, not only embarrassed by Jesus, whose doctrines they are incapable of putting into practice, but turned into the everyday cantors of Judaism, the artisans of Israel's eternity.

A man who mumbles and pulls on his beard for two hours is someone who has more than one trick up his sleeve.

* * *

The airplane banks heavily to the left, goes into a nose dive, jumps for joy three times, comes to a stop. The door opens, the stairs are brought up. We get off...

Rome! A warm wind embraces you as soon as you set foot on the stairs. It welcomes you as a friend. A brilliant sun, an old, wise sun that knows neither how to bite nor to scratch. A hospitable star. Translucent weather, product of a deep and pure sky, speckled by a few sparse, still, white clouds. We don't sufficiently understand that wind, sun, days, nights, are somewhat the same throughout the world because in other places we adorn them with so many marvelous colors. I would have hoped that, in Rome, the day could have another shade than ours so as to give me the happy illusion of being in another world.

Roma! pronounced as the indigenous people pronounce it, the city's name has a musicality which lies between a caressing whisper, an incantation and an order. It stays in you, provoking waves which attach you to the environment more. On huge billboards, a national brand beverage greets you in the name of the entire country. *Cinzano.* Is it a warning? A proverb? Am I being put on guard against my own weaknesses, against a somewhat exaggerated taste for alcohol? Or do they want to point out that, of all beverages, Cinzano is the least harmful? I understand. When a Roman invites me to his home, I would be ungracious not to drink Cinzano, with temperance, and if he happened to come to my home, not to offer it to him with intemperance.

How long has it been there, this sign, in the forefront of the great struggle to sweep the consumers off their feet, to get the lion's share of the business and to break the rivals' back, doing them in so as to be the only one to breathe the air earmarked for millions of people? Am I going to find exacerbated here in Rome the selfishness I glimpsed among other peoples? Is man going to be used for the benefit of certain companies just as he is elsewhere? Struggle! Fortune! Me! and no one else! Is this really the first lesson that Rome can give to me? The only trade mark, the only people? A chosen people, a first-class people, authorized to step on everyone else, in the shadow of the cross?

I refuse to believe that of a holy city. And yet, this equatorial blossoming of propaganda boards—made of enamel to withstand the weather—has a deep meaning for me. It is the symptom of a disease, the sign of an attitude, the most obvious indication of a desire for power.

Roma!

Have the merchants who were chased from the original temple found shelter and good land? What relationships do they have with the huge dome that stands out against the sky as if attesting, night and day, to the actual presence of Him who, multiplying bread and fish, distributed them freely?

Are there less tears in Rome than there are at home and among other people? Does the mandarin orange tree have a suitable bed? Does man, as a man, have the rights inherent in his nature? The wind caresses my cheek as if to tell me to calm down, to wake up, to convince me that Rome is a city inhabited by men and not by angels. I would really like to know what the old rabbi, who smiles at me as he mumbles, is thinking about. I don't know. He casts a proud glance over everything, the glance of a master who seems to mock what he sees. He seems to insinuate by his whole attitude that it still is and always will be the era of the merchants in the temple. A guide comes to escort us to customs. The room appears tiny to one who is still haunted by the vision of Paris' large, bright rooms. And why this kind of box in front of which the customs officers move about and who to me seem like priests extending their hand to show the catechumens into the temple after the formalities? Beforehand, the police had initialed our papers. Any traveler who didn't seem to have permission to enter into the holy city is put on the index. Men keep watch over the gates of their city. The old walls, widened and enlarged, still have lookouts at every corner.

The customs desk. My turn. I expected the routine question: "What do you have to declare?" as I opened my suitcase, a question which, here, would have meant: "What do you want, what are you looking for by coming to Rome? What do you expect from Rome as you knock at her door? Be welcome if you come with a pure and unbiased heart."

With no forewarning, not even the slightest smile, even as I continued to bless his Parisian counterpart, the Roman customs officer seizes a piece of big white chalk and says:

—Tabac?[15]
—Tabac?
—Yes, tabac.
—What tabac?
— Do you have some tobacco?

—Some tobacco?

I stared at him to make him understand that I didn't understand. I held out all my money. This customs agent didn't look at it. I counted the bills, he didn't see them. He seemed not to place any importance on Parisian money. With a gesture of his hand he made me understand that that didn't much interest him. It is not a Roman customs agent's job to give chase to Parisian money. I show him money and he questions me about tobacco! What a funny country! To be a Roman is really to be of another species. I'm beginning to understand why the old rabbi looked at everything from on high. It's only then that one can seem indulgent. This man, at the outside doors of the city, didn't ask me if I carried any gold, alcohol or drugs, but tobacco! As if tobacco were a precious commodity.

I raised my arms and then patted my suit-pockets to show that I wasn't carrying any tobacco.

Continuing to dig through my suitcase, the Roman customs officer discovers two very sweet smelling pineapples. He looks at me.

—Ananas...I say.

—Nanasse.

—No, ananas.

—Ananasse?

—Yes...

I will learn later that all the letters in a word are pronounced. Auto becomes a-oto. Is this a sign that everyone in this country must effectively play his role? Contribute to the proper functioning of the city without his origin, the color of his beliefs, the form of his thought being taken into account? A solid unity having as its goal the happiness of everyone?

The customs officer marks a cross on my suitcase. This sign permits me to leave the airport. I'm allowed to penetrate into Rome.

A great joy comes over me. Here I am in Rome! the holy city, my spiritual home! I'm going to walk in the footsteps of illustrious predecessors, contemplate the same sky that they did, breathe the same air filled with the same perfumes! I dare not look around me too much. But how can I contain a joy that is spreading through me? I try just the same to adopt a certain air of indifference that probably fools no one. Eyes fix themselves on me. A black in Rome—undoubtedly that doesn't happen everyday. An event, then? However, the men, if I'm not mistaken, seem less curious than the Parisians, or do they just have another way of observing you which is more discreet than the Parisians! As for myself, with our inborn naiveté, I look them straight in the eyes. Those whom I stare at like that merely smile. A good sign!

In front of the customs post is the office of a credit establishment whose gold sign shines indiscreetly: *Banco di Santo Spirito*, Bank of the Holy Spirit. What surprises Rome has in store for me! After the Cinzano look-out posts mounting guard on the runway, after the customs-officer-tobacco-digger, here is the Bank of the Holy Spirit! Everything here is just blended together! In order to understand my surprise, I have to tell you that in the religion of the Romans and Parisians, the one which I adopted, God is one being in three persons: the Father, the Son and the Holy Spirit. This is the first of the great mysteries, that is to say facts that man cannot explain to himself and must not even attempt to explain. Thus, the Holy Spirit completes the Father and the Son. It partakes of the two; and all three, bound together at all times, are one. Now, Jesus Christ the Son came upon the earth to reconcile men with the Father because of a very old story about the forbidden apple eaten by Adam, everyone's ancestor; Jesus Christ supposedly declared that no one could serve God and Mammon at the same time. Mammon was his name for money, according to the linguists. He even went much further by affirming that it would be more difficult for a rich person to go to Paradise than for an elephant to pass through the eye of a needle. A formal condemnation of money and of wealth by the Father, the Son and also by the Holy Spirit. In those times, men were shaken by it. Fortune was the only means of distinction, of classification. To put a curse upon the rich was to undermine the foundations of the society. Jesus Christ can have fun distributing bread, fish and wine since his kingdom is not a part of this world, but those who have made this earth their fatherland, those who possess nothing anywhere else and who wonder if there is another universe somewhere beyond the clouds, judging that he disturbed their peace, nailed him on a cross, his large arms open as if inviting him to receive the poor and the unhappy who were anxious to join him. The poor and the unhappy never raised a finger to manifest their desire to join Christ. The rich people concluded from this that reason was on their side and Mammon, put back on his pedestal, continued to rule the lives of millions of people.

Centuries have passed. Men have evolved. With God the Father still in the sky and God the Son nailed to the Cross, the very astute Romans, seeking to reconcile the irreconcilable, found it timely, beneficial, political to house God the Holy Spirit in a bank, the house of Mammon. They asked him to keep watch over what Jesus had condemned. Wealth and faith, housed in the same temple, are undoubtedly at the service of the same class, the descendants of those who judged Jesus' teachings to be outrageous. Has money become a holy spirit? the invigorating spirit, young vigorous blood running through the veins of the Roman people? Has it preserved its corruptive power, the evil power which, at home, allows it to win lost causes? *Banco di Santo Spirito!* Is this to indicate that money, spirit of the modern world, should play a more human role from now on? Uniting men, families, peoples and nations instead of dividing them into poor and rich? Serving to develop rather than to stifle? Mammon, not divinized, but tamed, subjugated to the whims of men who turn it into a revitalizing material. I think the sign must be understood in this light because, at first sight, Rome seems too human to me for it to be otherwise.

Why do all those people who are leaving the bank window have a smile? What inner fire illuminates them, sweeps them off their feet? How their walk has changed! And their eyes, why are they projecting those strange flames? It's as if they have all become mere machines. What beneficent rays is the window giving off? What power is bathing them, all these customers? I would like my turn not to come so as to observe this phenomenon better. But I suddenly find myself in front of the window, my heart pounding, hands moist and drops of sweat on my back. In my mind, forgetting that I am Roman by belief, I call upon all our gods to come stave off the bad fortune. The employee gives me bank notes of a thousand and five hundred francs, which in size are double the Parisian paper money. And suddenly everything starts to spin around me. I feel like a new man. In handling them I feel a kind of ecstasy and power. They fill up my hands, speak to me in an unknown language which could make me commit the most foolish acts. I walk like the others, head high, like an automaton, torso straight, arms held away from the body to show my importance. The men who are seated or who come and go seem like dwarfs to me. However tall, big and strong they may be, they don't have these bills that I have, these bills which appeared suddenly in the gay sky and which are really the characteristic signs of the spontaneity, exuberance, intemperance and display that undoubtedly constitute the basis of Roman mentality. In the shadow of the bank of the Holy Spirit, you can't help but talk loudly and gesticulate a lot! The Parisians haven't yet realized this marvelous effect of Roman money when they maintain that the people here talk not only with their eyes, mouth and chin, but especially with their hands.

It's a miracle that the entire body doesn't imitate the dance. For I feel strange tinglings in me and I gesticulate with pleasure. I'm on pitch. Everything is bubbling in me and, like the first apostles, I'm ready to speak all the languages of the world...This limpid and clear sky, this warm sun as on a windy morning, and these bank notes from the Holy Spirit!

I admit I've never had so much confidence in myself! Ever since I began hearing the light noises in my inner pocket, the very special rustling, ever since the strange power of Roman money started rising within me, I feel as if I have wings. Happy and with full hands, happy a thousand times over!

I understand the precaution that the Roman customs officer took by asking me if I had any cigarettes. With the intoxication that the bills from the Bank of the Holy Spirit bring on, one is capable of provoking catastrophies just by throwing away cigarette butts. The luminous and dry weather seems highly inflammable.

I could no longer say whether or not the bank sign was gilded, what color the teller's hair was, whether or not he had gold teeth like most of his Parisian counterparts. The liras had charmed, dazzled and stunned me.

The line was formed without any scuffle and the Parisian travelers, very urbane, forgot to insist upon "their place," "their turn." The Bank of the Holy Spirit had worked its first miracle on the Parisians.

A woman with black hair, dressed in a black skirt and a bodice in the same shade, invites me to ride in a luxurious bus, one of those tall buses which carry the tourists around in Paris. It's new and shining. You'd think it just came from the factory. Two men on the side of the vehicle greet me demonstratively. I get on. Each of the upholstered seats has a landscape on the back. Now that's intelligent propaganda, by no means flashy. No language. No obtrusive commentary. Artists, psychologists, these Romans are! They put you in front of the landscape, it's up to you to judge, to appreciate, to decide...freely. These regions are undoubtedly of such world-wide repute that their praises are no longer sung. That's left up to the numerous tourists and to all the newlyweds from the white world who come here to live the first happy days of their union. Rome's sky must have the power to reinforce the ties of the heart. To make your stay pleasant, a thousand hands lure and push you into a mechanism that functions to perfection. After the invitation to drink Cinzano, there is the one to visit the region. The Roman, with an unparalleled cleverness, excites the traveler's curiosity. He lays out before the latter the whole gamut of his landscapes.

I finally understand why the Parisian authorities are so strict about allowing each passenger only twenty thousand francs. Rome could become an abyss for French wealth. With the fidgets the Parisian suffers from and the excessive love he feels for Rome, dams had to be erected so that the Tiber wouldn't wash away all the riches from the Seine.

* * *

Here, the women seem smaller than the Parisian women; they have shinier teeth and slightly flat noses. The thickness of the air must be the cause of this kind of nose, which tends to resemble ours. Solidly built, full of life, that's apparent in their walk, their sometimes haughty gestures, their readily authoritative voices; they open their mouths more when talking, and hearing them I have the impression of hearing water falling on gravel and making it roll. A musical language, very musical, even more musical in the mouths of women who seem to embellish it with their smile and with the flame of their gaze. And how well they speak their language, the women! To hear them, you would think that they're going to run out of breath! Wrong. They can converse for hours on end at the same pace without running out of breath. They would be so much the healthier for it. Just like all the women in the world. The Roman women stare at you without insolence.

They seem to have acquired an absolute consciousness of their value. Men and women come and go with ease, with the feeling of being the masters of their country, the inheritors of the past, and the artisans of the future. In this regard, Rome is not a country that will let itself be dominated by its machines, by the number of its war vessels; the people are too alive, too open to nourish and persevere in aggressive schemes. The stream of great Roman conquests has withdrawn to its bed.

Is there a man in the country who can speak without being heard? Are they all deaf? Here they don't whisper into your ear as they do in Paris where everything seems to be marked top secret. Is the Roman citizen more free? Does Rome accord possibilities for development to each individual? Are the men so exuberant because they are satisfied with their government? Under the Roman sky, peopled by small white clouds just like the down fallen from the wings of little angels, does liberty have a broader meaning, to the point of instilling in each individual a more acute sense of his own value, of his responsibilities? In any case each man sits straight in his chair, speaks firmly to make himself well understood and to show that in the Empire of the Bank of the Holy Spirit, since the miracle of Pentecost, man is born with the gift of speech. I will even see waiters serving to the rhythm of popular songs.

When the people here call out to each other, I have the impression of being back home. In Paris, this way of shouting would have been shocking. The Parisian is atrophied by wanting to be temperate in everything, to calibrate everything, weigh and maintain everything, cultivating the numerous conformities upon which his existence is erected as a house is constructed on piles. Every kind of noise flusters the Parisian who seems to live on the edge of a life in which the Roman moves with frightening ease. The latter seems to accord the same meaning to life that we do. Thus, it's not surprising that so many hit songs see the light of day on the banks of the Tiber where music impregnates everything with an almost palpable presence. Here, indulgence seems easy to obtain. That explains certain abuses that were made of it in the past. Your heart is won over by the sight of such beautiful bosoms and of shapes that can be compared to the shapes from home. I asked myself all kinds of questions... Traveling doesn't form just the young, it also forms the old; and each day I understand more completely, in its most subtle sense, the precept which teaches us to treat our neighbor as we would have him treat us. At first sight, nothing deep or racial separates me from the Roman. Our differences could have come from our forests, our perspectives, our education. I feel just as close to him as to the Parisian. The education we received has prepared us for this meeting, for this deep and real appreciation, for this authentic assessment of man. And our kind of life, our conception of the world also. I watch all these men coming and going, I hear them laugh, I see them tease each other, pinch a friend, trounce each other, which makes the others laugh. Exactly what we do when we're together.

Skin colors are abolished as soon as we observe each other from a certain angle and, on that level, we feel the hunger and thirst of others. Any difference? None, with all due respect to those who consider themselves born to be masters; we're the products of our governments, and often the unconscious actors for others' interests.

A country where men are so alive, where women can laugh loudly, where sky is so blue, pure and deep, the wind so roguish, can only be inclined to indulgence; it understands all the weaknesses of the heart. For this wind is so gentle, so special; it carries such indefinable scents, such powers that you would like to take off your jacket and shirt to feel it on your skin.

The bus has started off. Slowly. Along the route, billboards serve as sentries announcing Roman products. In our villages, going from street to street, we advertise our merchandise by word of mouth. The Roman entrusts this job to billboards. Very economic and astute system. We appeal to the ear, he to the eyes, because the men on the banks of the Tiber not only speak their language but also enjoy the privilege of being able to write it. Priceless advantage for a people who have a soul that they intend to save and values to enrich by contact with other men. They don't fear meetings, confrontations; if not, would they make such strong propaganda efforts to attract people to their country? Moreover, I don't think that they want to convert people. Rome no longer has its old vitality, you can feel it by the gait of the citizens, by the power of the wind and in addition, by the stunted, old grass, which extends as far as the eye can see. Degenerated grass...

Too much history has happened here not to weigh upon the man, not to constitute for them a hard kind of shell that is difficult to crack. History, passing with time, has left its dregs upon the earth, upon the country. Are the inhabitants demarcated, restricted, like the earth?

Coquettish houses along the way. A new style is born. Puddles of water, here and there, cement blocks in uncovered piles; to the side, a spade and a shovel... Exactly what happens at home. The negligence of some, the incompetence of others is so onerous for public finances. The citizen must not be satisfied with the government under which he's living. These negligences are signs of it. There exists here, as among other peoples, a scientifically organized oligarchy, a well-provided-for minority, and a majority toeing the line. And the discontented worker avenges himself by leaving a sack of cement and work tools out in the open. How exciting it is to play with the public wealth! And I dream about open sewers that are never closed and badly lit at night, about trucks stopped without any lights on a curve, about official cars which are put in service on the first of the month to be smashed into bits two weeks later.

After all, without these small, dearly bought fantasies, wouldn't life be monotonous? If we didn't continue to entertain the people by burning up millions in fireworks, wouldn't they be the first to consider themselves abandoned? And that is how certain people, through a diabolical skill, have been successful in hoisting themselves on the shoulders of a people. Does Rome still have solid shoulders? How many kings, courtesans' favorites is she holding? And for how many more years can she support them?

Always being careful, thinking about your neighbor. What's the use when this old people from an old civilization doesn't seem to have succeeded in giving its workers a more precise notion of their duties? I presume that they are all thrown pell-mell into the work force where the most deserving are not always the best paid. The paradox, in these countries where the roads are beautiful and straight, is that in order to deal in business, man seems to be forced to follow labyrinthian channels, to get lost in the footpaths and undergrowth of laws; at every turn someone is there to demand some kind of tribute. No one complains. This practice gives charm to their existence. It's one of its attractive sides.

In the country, old towers dot the way, watch towers which served to give the alert to the old Romans. When an enemy approached the State's boundaries, high flames, from tower to tower, warned Rome. These ruins are still erect, as are those of the aqueducts. Integrated ruins which probably signify Rome's will never to break with its past. No head of state has dared to demolish them... Precious vestiges, they're the first monuments that the traveler sees. They remain there to say how old Rome is and to what extent time can triumph over human works. How many tears they must have caused to be shed! How many mothers have they made tremble! And how many agonized prayers have been said, in hovels, so that men might stop trembling!

And we still tremble the world over!

These ruins fiercely resist time, which degrades them a little each day, as if to liberate dreams, the souls of those who died on the job. Those who built them, those who inaugurated them with enthusiasm, those who came running from all provinces to admire them, all of them are dead. The ruins remain, simple traces in time.

A lesson in humility, modesty, wisdom. Rome leaves them there intentionally, at the city's entrance, so that everyone will not only contemplate them, but understand them and know that he is penetrating a sanctuary, in a city peopled with ghosts, full of relics and superstitions.

In addition, isn't the harmonizing of the past and present the mark of a temperate people?

I have never encountered men who knew how to camouflage the truth so well. By the ruins spread out along the road, they would like to make me believe that they are the oldest people in the world. Certainly, the child who has only tasted his mother's sauce never knows that he can find better sauces elsewhere. This proverb from home applies wonderfully to the Roman case. Now that I have set foot in this land, they must understand their error, for our color attests that we are the first race to see the light of day. All the others can wait until the sun has had the time to "smoke their skin." I proudly show off mine as the universe's oldest monument. But these Romans, crassly ignorant, accord me no importance, convinced as they are that the only valuable monuments for the entire world are the ruins left by their ancestors. The astonishing thing is that no one points them out to you.

Two large butterflies on the billboard fly to meet us. It's the first time I've ever encountered such a symbol at a city's entrance. After the ruins, here are the butterflies: "the chickens of paradise". Does Rome know that she has just unveiled herself amost completely? The Eternal City, it knows how to blend the lightness, the caprices of the butterfly with the rigorous demands of the modern city.

Rome knows how to dream, how to put men at ease. Rome invites you to flutter, to leap right into daily existence.

People often think that to understand a city or a nation it is important to interview various inhabitants or to run from library to library. Not always the most fruitful method for those who have a "skin"and eyes, and who know how to interpret what they feel and see on the road leading to the city. They proceed exactly like hunters on the prowl, distinguishing the noise of a twig falling of its own accord from that of a branch an animal has brushed against. This method allows you to trace a people's evolution and to know its tastes. Nations bare their souls in everything that embellishes their city or their homes. Thus, in order to soften the harsh lines of contemporary buildings, Parisians hang climbing plants on the walls. They bring trees and birds into their rooms and in so doing reaffirm their contact with other creatures. A fad, undoubtedly, but with a profound meaning...Their splendid isolation has begun to weigh upon them; the leveling and squaring, their whole mode of reasoning (How? Why? Therefore!) have not been able to give them a true understanding of existence.[16] Europe has finally understood this elementary truth: man is more than an individual trained to think only about comfort, a being constantly apprehensive and ready for any compromise, any dissimulation in order to hold a position, play a role or wear a mask. Man of his own accord is replacing himself in the natural environment, which he should never have left. Now Europe, as if to teach a lesson, to point out the right road, not only tries to maintain contact with the sun, the water, the air, the trees, but pushes this thirst for "communal-unity" to the point of transforming her homes into gardens and of liberating man from the oppressive harshness of certain imperatives which she judges to be out-of-date or at least unadaptable to the present century.

"Hotel Regina Coelli." Hotel of the Queen of Heaven!

Cinzano, butterflies, ruins, hotel of the Queen of Heaven, Bank of the Holy Spirit, and reigning over it all, the sun, a sweet, warm sun in a limpid sky.[17] This is Rome!

Let someone tell me that the day breaks on this city first and I would willingly believe it, for everything seems so new, joyous, full of life, spirit, gaity, and good-heartedness.

In the airplane, the beautiful jagged outlines of the coast had already impressed me. And the blue of the ocean, which seems to be resting from a long journey. This country could only be a country of relaxation and of lovers. What seems unbelievable is that men agree to work when everything encourages idleness: the earth, the grass, the flowers, the mountains, the cross-roads, the splendid highways. Dreaming people living off investments, mixing love and spirit with everything they undertake. People who are at once artistic and obstinate, inherited qualities from the past; traders, also, right to their very fingertips.

Over there, to the distance, a powerful dome surmounted by a globe holding a cross stands out in profile. This is the Pope's domain. God's representative on earth, the father of all those who believe and pray to God in Roman fashion, that's to say with oriental ostentation. Jesus Christ supposedly lived in shameful poverty. Luckily, the Bank of the Holy Spirit was born; and God could be served by men dressed so as to command the respect of Mammon's faithful.

That Jesus should abolish customs, that could be tolerated; that he should preach that we treat others like ourselves, that could be allowed, but that he should speak of a Father mocking wealth seemed like a monstrosity. And I suspect Rome of walking in the footsteps of the rabbi's ancestors, especially since our Roman god has a fortified city, built on the model of worldly cities, without omitting draw-bridges and look-out windows. At the entrance to the only door is found a vigilant guardian named Saint Peter who is at the same time God's head servant. Many persons here think that taking Peter as a first name will make him less rigorous at their hour of death. A God of the citadel! Of the clan!

Christ thought that men would be more considerate of each other if they had the same God. The message of brotherhood as it passed over borders and continents took on a macabre quality because it was put in the service of frightful interests. And so, in several places, Jesus was constrained to preside over judgments leading to the stake: proud and courageous creatures defended God whose patience enraged them. They sent his prodigal sons off to him by force so that He would not have to kill the fattened sheep for them.

Ardent faith! and religious intoxication, that they now temper by lodging god and the devil together. And they seem to make a happy couple in Rome, judging by the power I feel since I have the lira from the Bank of the Holy Spirit on my person. When one has so many ruins around him and in him, one tries to reconcile the irreconcilable. Rome has reached that point.

* * *

The bus finally stops for the last time. We're at the Termini station, one of the wonders of Roman architecture. The Roman proves to be a builder and is anxious to remain the authentic descendant of those who constructed aqueducts and high defensive walls, which time seemed to regret destroying. Termini Station? A long gallery of windows framed in metal.

Pronto!

What a marvelous station! Did I let some exclamation fall from my lips, since eyes are darting at me. I must have been myself for a moment.

Pronto!

Here, one must avoid behaving in an African way, that is spontaneously, exuberantly, and naturally. It's not civilized. Every movement must be mastered, analyzed, then controlled. The heart is subordinated to reason. It is too busy beating night and day to maintain any lucidity in its reactions. The world of reason could not possibly be affective, and every habit, every gesture which doesn't fit in or have an accepted place, passes for something strange and unusual, and if mouths keep themselves from shouting it, eyes won't hesitate to make you understand.

Drowned in this crowd, crushed and pushed around by people in a hurry, I turn towards one of the huge exit doors. Bars, book stores, perfume merchants, a little of everything that is sold in the city is gathered together at the station, in front of the customers. Souvenir stores where portraits of the Holy Father the Pope are sold. Another flowering industry. God's representative on earth is sold in all forms and constitutes the most important item for certain vendors. I understand the rabbi's haughtiness: In Rome also, they still sell God at public auctions. Gold and silver, having once again attained prominence, have enslaved man and penetrated into the most respectable of citadels.

Rows of boothless telephones and one hears men and women, serious and smiling, calling Pronto! Pronto! Are all Romans named Pronto? Wait, this is the equivalent of the Parisian "Allò." Where does this expression come from and what does it mean exactly?

It's in Rome that I ask myself the question, because until then, I had thought that all European people, when picking up their phone, began their sentence with "Allò!" A conventional expression accepted by everyone. An international word. That's not the case at all. To "Allò," Rome has preferred "Pronto," which must have special meaning for her. What exactly? Is it the need to maintain originality?

"How big a foreigner's eyes are."* That's my situation. I open mine wide

*Proverb which means that a foreigner must have everything explained to him.

75

and see hardly anything. Allô! for me meant: "Is this really you?" "Oh, how happy I am to be talking to a human! Let's keep in touch."

The mania for phoning is terrifying, just as terrifying as it is in Paris. It's the sign that the individual here also leads a mutilated life, even when he controls millions. The language of lira doesn't completely replace human language. And we are right to say that "man is an older brother to money." We have priority in every situation. This role couldn't be inverted because God created man who, in turn, thought about money. Now it seems that man is serving the younger brother who makes unreasonable demands because his heart is also drunk with power.

In this regard, we are very different from the Roman. None of the tall buildings impress me since the men they house are diminished, bridled, arrested in their development.

Or on the contrary, does Rome constitute a large family where everyone is aware of everyone else's secrets, a country with walls made of glass?

Pronto! here, Pronto! there...Pronto! everywhere... upon arrival, upon leaving, between two glasses of beer, between two errands? Men who consult their watches and run toward the telephone. How can the Roman keep up this hellish pace? It doesn't seem to jibe with his temperament, which is so much like ours.

On the lower level of the station, stores are lined up.

Pronto! One has the impression that Rome lives glued to the telephone, waiting, in its capacity of holy city, for a message which doesn't come. And the street cars pass, crammed with men who try to smile, as if they carried good news. An incessant coming and going. More in tempo with man, more human, more poetic than Paris. Undoubtedly, Rome would like someone to help her get rid of the steel-wire webs that spoil her beauty, that the street-cars be abolished, the rails removed from the street, these vestiges from another age. But who, in Rome, would dare to touch these relics? When right next to the station are other ruins named the Servius Tullius Walls. These walls existed several years before Christ was born. The Roman who is caught between these walls and this unique station can have strange attitudes towards others. He must reconcile the past, which observes him from all sides, and the present, which solicits him.

In front of the station is the Piazza dei Cinquecento. Square of the Five Hundred Soldiers. According to history, Rome, forgetting that she had aged, and thus misjudging her powers, got into a dispute with an African nation over something trifling: a few acres of land. Elders are sometimes aggressive, the last stand against decrepitude. Rome undoubtedly scorned the wise advice that her neighbors didn't hesitate to offer. On the first day of conflict, she lost five hundred fighters, five hundred new heroes. Men who, while still alive, were dying probably from hunger. Now the nation cherished them. A disaster, a national shame; that this calamity could happen when they were attacking a well-armed European nation can be understood, but that it should be inflicted by a somewhat unsophisticated tribe seemed strange. The other States took the defeat humorously. They are in the habit of doing that. While consoling their unhappy neighbor, they didn't stop telling and retelling her:

—And then, you could have been more prudent.

—After all, you just don't come to blows with a horde!

—What business did you have laughing with those barbarians?

—Where else does it hurt you? In the back? Ah, those savages! Reducing you to such a state.

So much so that a veiled anger mounted in Rome. These false-hearted consolations were like salt in the wounds. She knows that in such cases you're supposed to turn the other cheek. She didn't want to for fear of losing her teeth. You never know with these savages! So, she preferred to resort to the sword.

At home, the elders, as soon as they had returned from the battle, would have left no stone unturned in looking for the meaning of the catastrophe; women would have danced entire nights to appease the angry gods. The Abyssinians would have been only instruments of the angry gods. The slaughter of countless sheep and chickens would have occurred.

The Romans, on the other hand, acknowledged the blow and, not being a vengeful people, gave the name of Piazza dei Cinquecento to this very animated square so that each citizen, whether entering or leaving Rome, so that each child held by a mother would know that there is an honor to save, there is a sore on the wolf's forehead, a wound waiting to be cleaned, and flowers to be put on graves.

National defeats being unbearable, how wise it would be for diplomats to conform to our proverb that says: "The good courtesan, the best diplomat is the one who partially executes the orders of an angry king." If he orders the burning of a village, you should be content to set fire to grass at the entrance to the agglomeration. For he can go back on his decision. On this side of the ocean, the specialists who are always at work dream only of increasing their power and being used to the bonfires on the feast of Saint John, they like to see large, purifying flames. Fire has a diabolical role on this continent.

I don't know if the African tribe extols this victory every year on the day Rome cries for its dead, or if the sounds of the drum coming from beyond the sands and the ocean add their notes to the concert of resentment, their drop of water to hearts being filled with bitterness. Rome suffered this defeat in the name of all the peoples of her color who, while acting as if nothing had happened, no longer included it among the great powers. To be beaten by blacks, during the period of great European expansion, at a time of mechanical and technological supremacy, was a notorious sign of weakness, incapacity, regression and decadence. People deliberately closed their eyes to prestigious Roman history, to what the country had been able to give to the world, in order to better shed light upon the defeat at the hands of a savage tribe. So, before the cautious mocking concert of nations—and God knows how these people make fun of men—each Roman, when crossing the Piazza dei Cinquecento, blushed before all of Europe. Discriminated against, Rome reached the point of no longer cherishing her venerable ruins; she no longer understood their language. Even those of Servius Tullius no longer meant anything to her. Rome seemed to have broken with a past which in all situations allowed her to aim for prudence, wisdom, which allowed her to plunge herself into time, history and to come up with a reasonable solution, that is to say, a human one. The old Rome fell into the ranks of the young nations possessing neither aqueducts, public baths nor the Servius Tullius ruins. The Christian city, for the national honor, charitably pondered its reverence while forging bayonets, constructing planes and making dum-dum bullets...—special bullets for infidels, designed to pulverize skins in order to show God to what extent his creatures exalted the brotherhood that united them. If a collective delirium took hold of Rome, the fault lay with the savage tribe which had lacked tact. It's traditional for old people to correct children. The contrary calls down the curse...Those are African customs. So?...An intolerable gesture not to be left unpunished. If it were, the foundations of society would be destroyed. Often a State conducts itself like an individual and Rome, rejuvenated, let herself be carried away by the music of her arsenals, forgetting her role as mediator in world affairs, a role that was hers by right of her millenial experience. The Roman gods, accustomed to not being insulted must have been among those who would find it most difficult to forgive. At the outset, fabulous goods, valuable perfumes, rare gold had been promised to them, and what was brought back? A jacket. And what a jacket! It was so ugly that they themselves were angry with the adversary for having resisted. They remained hungry. And when gods are hungry, men go crazy...Piazza dei Cinquecento.

From window to window, I penetrate into the fortress without anyone having asked for either my quay or my train ticket. I carry the audacity to the point of getting in a first class coach; still no one to tell me anything. Strange people! So here I am far, really far, very far from Paris, with its thousands of check points and toll-gates! I understand to what extent Paris is a money-grubber, finicky, stingy, always collecting money; Rome still wears the toga and has majestic gestures. The ancient contacts she had with the continent opposite her have marked her somewhat. And how can you be surprised after such feats that Rome is a poor city? Undoubtedly, the inhabitants are more builders than tax-collectors and thus give to men and to the foreigner a greater illusion of liberty. The political regime is undoubtedly more flexible: the leaders can hardly conceive that a train station built with public funds cannot be visited by every Roman, so they can see what has been done with the different taxes demanded of them.

The fact that Paris multiplies barriers and that Rome limits them is food for thought. The blindness that leads to imitating everything, to adopting from Paris, London and New York both their accent and their tics, is a sign of weakness and proves to what extent a people can underestimate itself. Thus, many young nations, dazzled by the display of appearances, anxious to enjoy life at the risk of demeaning themselves, don't want to be born in pain. How can there be births without pregnancies? The others of us, happy people without a history, follow, unruffled, the path our ancestors have traced for us. No cloud in our sky. God is with us and we unceasingly call upon him throughout our never-ending discussions. He alone knows hearts. If it appears that an ambitious person carves out the lion's share for himself, that's only an exception, because the people, conscious of the fairness of the positions, follow with patience and obstinacy. They follow, because if they were to precede, the leader would have the devil in his purse, so shrewd, economical and covetous are the people. No more sacrifices? And the leader's job wouldn't be profitable. For the moment, the people are asked to be faithful, to remain faithful, to follow, keeping their eyes fixed on the one who precedes. Fidelity doesn't need to be lucid: this would be harmful. The only thing that matters is that it be pervasive and solid as a rock.

So our country is a sanctuary without any discord in its daily prayer. To all the questions that can be asked, the best response is "Amen" so that in a cloud of incense and praises, the capital in transit will continue to honor us with its comforting presence. These capital investments, moreover, are always directed through the same channels and knock on the same doors. Fussy guests, they have a weakness for buildings situated on heights.[18] A clear view allows them to scrutinize the horizon and watch for the dominant wind. In the lowlands swarming with people, they would be treated with less respect.

Actually, we don't know how well-off we are. You have to travel in order to measure how much distance there is between us and the others. I was unable to appreciate our grandeur until after I had crossed the boundaries of our powerful state.

Some individuals still dare to affirm that traveling educates only young people. It also educates old people, especially when, like me, they have grown up in their sheltered world, worshipped the same god, danced the same dances and walked along the same footpaths that their ancestors did. What amazement! What an affirmation of the self as an individual and as a nation!

* * *

To get to the hotel, I take a taxi which is standing near the station. Evening is approaching and the meter on the inside isn't lit. I hold out the address. The driver takes off, makes a thousand detours down brightly lit streets and through wasteland of sorts. I begin to wonder if I'm not taking another trip just as long as the one from Paris to Rome, when suddenly the taxi stops. The driver looks at the dashboard, throws me the figures. I serve up a bill from the wad that I carry next to my heart. He feels it, holds it between his fingers for a moment as if to capture its beneficial powers. And that does it! He smiles. He lays it down near him, turns his head toward me, looks at me, plunges his hand in his pocket, counts, recounts and hands me the change. Then he takes the bill, folds it slowly, undoubtedly ritualistically, and also puts it in his inner pocket, next to his heart. Now, I smile.

I feel like a Roman for having instinctively performed the same rites for goddess-lira. Has he taken the tip? How do we reach a man to man understanding even though we have the same considerations, the same fervour for the lira? Confidence reigns. It wouldn't occur to a native Roman to deceive an adopted Roman. To appease my conscience and undoubtedly to show that I know the customs of these shores, I hand him fifty lira. He looks at me, smiles again, and shakes his head negatively. Ah! What a country I've come to. Refuse a tip when everywhere else, it's demanded! You have to agree that all men on this continent haven't received the same education. Strange country where they have succeeded in quenching the thirst for profit by some sort of miracle. I'm looking for words to tell him that I have reserves of love and audacity in my heart; I have the desire, for a fraction of a second, to show him how much money I have with me; my lira turn my head. I put my hand in my pocket; I feel my bills and suddenly, I'm tempted to talk like the Romans. I whisper something and starting up the motor, the driver tells me: "Chào!" "Chào!" What can that mean? I throw his word back to him; he smiles and gestures in a friendly way. The word must not be very bad.

I find myself at the foot of a bronze statue, a few meters from the entrance of the hotel: "Caesar Augustus."

Caesar, in the language of one of the neighboring Punic countries, meant "elephant." What difference do you see between the Romans and us? Don't we have the elephant as an emblem? Don't our sovereigns call themselves elephants in order to give themselves more weight? To call oneself Lion, Tiger, Leopard, Elephant and then to maintain that man is superior to animals seems like an aberration to me. Or must we allow, to our great shame, that a chief has regressed when he names himself lion, tiger, leopard or buffalo? And along with him, all the people who submit to him. Thus it seems logical that such individuals embody the ferocity of their namesakes because they seem to have left the community of men for that of beasts. And, undoubtedly, that is why people still splash around in the mud of wars and wind through the labyrinths of misery. Certainly, it's high time they choose as leaders "men-chiefs" who are conscious of the worth of man's tears or of the explosive power of his smile. Chiefs who don't put themselves too much above others either, like new gods. Praises and prayers would have a disastrous effect and would bring them closer to their colleagues, the tiger, lion, or panther chiefs. Outside of his group man is in an unstable position and Roman wisdom consists in putting him in the hands of sanctified money, so that his madness for greatness will be holy madness, a madness that can be exorcized and is not bestial or demonic because it seems that, just like at home, money is the liquor that goes to your head most easily. And they have given this intoxication a very graphic name, "man-non," which in our language, n'zena, means "I haven't drunk." You don't drink money, you eat it as we say and it goes to your head. Even when you have it in an account, under your bed, in a bottle, it always goes to your head; keep it at a relative's house, very far away, it will still go to your head and will sometimes make you say things you shouldn't. Here, where the society is organized differently from yours but also where men have become conscious of the harmful effect of money on certain brains, they had only one reaction, to place it under the power of the Holy Spirit, in the care of all the angels, and this, with the holy intention of having money speak to each person in the language he can understand. As for me, I don't know whether the lira and I have really understood each other, but I admit with great shame –haven't I been taught to confess–that the lira's song makes me tipsy.

And getting back to Augustus who has men call him an Elephant, it must be acknowledged that men don't know much about each other even though they have the same dreams, the same appetites, under all skies and in all centuries.

* * *

The hotel is first class and the cook is preparing a meal said to be international, that is, a menu for all the stomachs of the world. Half-cooked rice, sugar in abundance, coffee, cakes, fruits. In vain I looked for something African, the waiters looked at me, astonished. I wanted some manioc, corn, bananas, some good papaya, yams. They didn't understand me. What more could one add to this international meal? In my naiveté, I forgot that we haven't yet entered the so-called international circuit; that Rome, in the international frame of reference, can only serve spaghetti just as Paris serves french fries, but no yams yet. And besides, why should I be so demanding, aren't I Roman by confession? Didn't I adopt spaghetti, one morning, on the threshold of a house where I chose a first name which hadn't yet been used in our country? And as if one of the waiters had followed my reasoning, he proceeded to place the smoking hot internationalized national dish in front of me: spaghetti. Ah, talk to me about it! spaghetti! Will I ever succeed in eating it the way my Roman brothers eat it?

In a very friendly manner, they had told me over and over again how to prevent my mistakes: "It's very simple; look, plunge your fork in the pile of pasta; then turn the fork around several times and you've got it!" I never succeeded. I plunged my fork in the pile, right in the middle, turned, turned, turned, but each time, as if to defy me, a rebellious pasta unwound just at the moment I stuck my mouth out like a bull-dozer ready to scoop up its mouthful of sand; this rebellious and unsociable pasta, bent on embarrassing me, had to fall on the napkin in spite of my discreet efforts to put it back on the plate. The first days, my stomach, which has its own special character, had difficulty accepting this international dish. It tried to maintain its identity. It didn't have any reason to change customs as I did. But who wouldn't change in Rome? Who wouldn't start dancing at the sound of the lira and with the help of the air, the sky and the weather, my stomach gave way to etiquette. It even developed a taste for spaghetti sprinkled with cheese. When the spaghetti appeared, I sighed with delight, I adopted a friendly attitude mixed with a bit of respect for the national dish. I had become completely Roman, from head to stomach. My feet stayed out of it, but a foot is made to obey; it's the people for the head, the anonymous crowd for the stomach. And my feet went along with it. I could have asked them to lead me into this city's most closed caste, the intellectual and university caste, and they would have done it. The age groups from back home are replaced here by professional groups which are impermeable to each other.

If social evolution at home is being accomplished without disruption, here, on the contrary, it is achieved by means of a struggle to the death against privileges which compel recognition. Whence the unstable character of the government. And the creation of castes. The intellectuals enjoy the privilege of distributing science and financiers that of favoring productivity while the politicians lead the country down a path foretold in advance. The priests have the duty of leading all these opposing creatures toward God. The most violent struggle is manifested between the university and the power structure. The latter thinks that too much light constricts its action, while the men of science affirm that light is so necessary that it was the first thing created by God. The argument is persuasive but not enough, however, to convince individuals who are accustomed to receiving homage. Then I ask myself a question: What could the university's role be at home, if by chance we decided to adopt some of the institutions of the peoples from these shores? Will it be an institution jealously guarding its privileges, or will it be a source of light? Will it educate men in the western tradition or men more strongly rooted in their own land? Certainly, it will have to defend itself against the abuses of power. It is that very struggle that will make it vigilant and conscientious.

* * *

Since yesterday some travelers who walk straight as a bamboo stalk have arrived at the hotel. They turn their heads with such pretentiousness that you would think they all had stiff necks. Rather tall, a darker white, they speak a language that not all the Romans understand. It seems they're English: citizens from an island in the middle of the sea, obstinate, stubborn men, proud of their "land," happy not to be from the continent. To show the difference, their car has the steering wheel on the right and they drive on the left; they drink full glasses of whiskey and take only water with meals. Very ceremonious men. They wear formal dress for meals and drink a small glass of fruit juice first. They have unctuous gestures. For them the meal is a holy act, a communion with the food and even with the cook. The tie they wear must serve to curb the audacity of the guzzlers. People open to all winds, exposed to all currents, knowing how to yield at the right moment, people who are ruthless in trading, ready to die for their island, and who in every way conform to their motto "God and my Rights." Their insularity is supposedly such that they don't care to speak the language of others. Their own suffices, and they think that it's the duty of other people to come to them. They would lose their footing if they left their island. The continent would swallow them up. Prudent people. I don't know if the lira could trouble their souls, but those I see stand so straight you would think they were insensitive to the insidious whispers of this Roman goddess. They are easily distinguished from the other guests in the hotel. Their insularity marks them, follows them, pursues them. It watches over them; while I, sometimes Parisian, sometimes Roman, could one day pass for a horrible chameleon or a common and abominable bat. And yet God knows from how many springs I can drink so that my feet won't be Parisian, or Roman, my stomach.

* * *

But who was this Caesar Augustus who is spoken so well of? He was one of the great people of this country, who covered their fatherland with glory and riches by cutting other people to bits. For us, Rome's history is full of lessons. They say that a certain Sylla, upon returning from Africa after a brilliant victory, marched on Rome to purge the city of all those who thought differently from him. For several weeks, his soldiers, who had learned their trade in Africa, with the odor of African blood still in their nostrils, and in their eyes, the glow of the flames of the enemy dwellings, killed deliriously, almost forgetting that they were killing brothers this time. Were those who thought differently from Sylla Romans? Could Sylla's bayonettes admit that anyone could think differently from him? One day, Sylla's soldiers captured a young man who had often been seen in the company of another consul, Marius, Sylla's adversary. They put a noose around his neck. Then, as they were about to strangle him, one of the soldiers, finding him too young, had him released.

This young man would go on not only to heap glory on Rome, but to bind Rome and Paris. Having become a general, he took up the idea of making vassals of the Romans, of proving how wisely the gods had acted in saving him in extremes. When he launched into the conquest of their country, the Parisians didn't at first understand what an honor he bestowed on them in bringing his armies onto their soil. We would have had the same reaction because you don't have to be Parisian to love your country. Attached to their customs, they refused the Roman yoke, which they found odious. The majority of Parisians rejected Roman money and the prestigious Roman civilization. Rome, through humanity, brought them her language, her customs, her way of thinking, her eagles covered with glory, her technicians, and these barbarians, through a limited sense of patriotism, opposed fraternization and the community of interests. They didn't appreciate the providential luck that having Romans within their walls represented for them. But a Roman's stubbornness exceeds a mule's and so with much patience and diplomacy, it happened that *vino, bambino, madre, rizoto, signori,* made themselves at home in the language and took on a Roman flavor by becoming *vin, bambin, mere, riz, seigneur.* The Roman triumphed. With wine once adopted, everything else would follow. In this delicious drink, the Parisian glimpses Truth. Its vapors gave him an approximate idea of what Roman grandeur was; that's the way it happened. At least, that's the way they tell it. Solidarity between Paris and Rome began with words. It was important to understand each other so that the Roman gold could work the final miracle. Rome's generosity being proverbial, giving her language, her customs and her gold wasn't enough. More had to be done in order to prove the disinterestedness which animated the legionaries who stood guard over the flags in the heart of Paris. Rome offered Paris a religion. The Parisians looked at their druids armed with golden sickles, they thought about their menhirs and dolmen. The legionaries looked at their pile of arms. In the sky, the clouds moved slowly by. Paris embraced the new religion with all the necessary enthusiasm. But Rome intended to benefit from her action. In the sky, the saints risked having short memories. She demanded that Paris retain the label on this religion and the epithet

"Roman" was affixed to it. Paris could say that things weren't quite that simple. It's possible, but can history be written differently? Would any State agree to commit suicide without masks and fireworks? So here is Paris, spiritually aboard the Roman slave-ship. Rome monopolizes the sky and makes a thousand demands of us if we want to attain God. She would like the Creator to speak and understand only Latin. In other words, every Christian should be perfectly at home in Rome. Unfortunately, this charitable spirit isn't understood by those who would like to speak to God in their own dialect. These barbarians forget that there is power in unity and that the same prayer said in the same language at the same hours acquires, with the help of weariness, an astonishing efficacy.

The statue of this illustrious man hardly seems kept up. Caesar Augustus, in the cold and in the heat! That's how far human recognition goes. Because he's now in bronze, nobody bothers about him. Because he can no longer distribute honors, people hardly look at him. Ah, if he could only come to life all of a sudden, how many men would wish to sprawl at his feet! But all that is asked of him is that he shade the business of a hotel with his shadow while not participating in the profits. Does Roman gratitude also end on the threshold of tombs?

"General or soldier, veteran or draftee, armed man whoever you are, stop here, and don't let the Rubicon be crossed either by your flags or by your arms, or by your army."

A very Roman statement leaving no way out. This imperious order had always restrained the boldest men of war. The Rubicon was not to be crossed. Only Caesar could dare to do it. Over what obstacles can an elephant not pass? Doesn't he become more bold when he feels threatened? Caesar, learning that he was going to be retired as the head of his legionaries, threw himself in the famous Rubicon shouting:

"Alea jacta est," "the die is cast." He didn't die from it. And this esteem shown by the gods added a new glory to his laurels. He could dare anything. From that day on the expression became popular and all those who make a decision, particularly those who wish to give themselves the air of a Caesar, whisper to themselves: "Alea jacta est." They cross an imaginary Rubicon.

This young man, who barely escaped hanging, wasn't about to restrict himself to breaking a law or to conquering the Parisians' ancestors in order to harness them to the Roman chariot. He pushed fearlessness to the point of disembarking upon the old African land that was so attractive to generals. A great western general will never consider himself authentic in his role if he hasn't done battle on African territory. The tradition is still alive. It's a muddy furrow in which they all like to wallow. The African gods, accustomed to these incursions, open an eye from time to time, in their drowsiness, as if to look at the time on the clock. They know how to wait. They were hardly troubled to hear Napoleon cry out: "Soldiers, from the top of these pyramids forty centuries are contemplating you." Calmly they watch soldiers transformed into anonymous dead whose names are forgotten by history. Insignificant addresses encumber her memory. And the African gods who know the names of all the vanished empires of all the war generals who came to struggle on their lands, add new names to those of the burned cities buried by the wind.

Nature abhors the blood and debris that mark the traces of men.

Upon returning from Africa, Caesar Augustus coined a famous saying. Addressing the Senate, he said: "Veni, Vidi, Vici!" I came, I saw, I conquered! Wasn't this a warning? When it suffices for a man to come and to see in order to conquer, that implies that everyone should submit. For us, this saying would have been food for thought. Here, it seemed so rare that the Romans stored it away among their treasures. They wouldn't make use of it anymore so as not to have the appearance of Caesars in a time when victories are doubtful. Since the drama of the Piazza dei Cinquecento, they have realized what weight they carry on their shoulders; even the good soldier gets disgusted with his job. Perhaps it's that, Caesar not having come to their aid in this new African adventure, they made a bellboy out of him in front of an international hotel. They seem to be saying to each guest: "Here is Caesar Augustus, the deserter!" He who knew Africa so well! He who carried mortal flames in his gaze! Where was he the day we walked in his tracks? By dint of reading and reciting his feats we had become little Caesars. Instead of being happy about it, he was jealous, he let us get bogged down in the marshes and stranded in the desert. A patriot? barely good enough to make a bellboy; so don't pity him. He was our most esteemed hero. We have brought him down from his pedestal to put him in the service of all. And Caesar Augustus plays the bellboy with a general's dignity. "There is no stupid job," says a Parisian proverb.

"Veni, Vidi, Vici!" The conciseness of the Roman sentence would lead you to believe that people here speak with their arms down at their sides. Luckily, that's not true at all because, thanks to the sun's gentle heat, they add a beautiful verbosity to the exuberance of authentic orators. This latter quality makes them like us. And I suspect them, although they deny it, of thinking in the same way we do. So is Caesar Augustus in the role of hunter anything to be shocked about? Isn't this a discreet warning to all of Caesar's apprentices? But who sees Caesar when the taxi leaves him at the hotel entrance? who bows to him? He has done his time. Consequently, he continues to play his role disdainfully. What legions of automatons is he commanding?

A music filled the room with its soft harmony.

But this general who never was wounded was to fall under the dagger of oblivious boys.

In power, he had struggled relentlessly against the privileges of certain families. These old parasites who still have disciples, judging the reforms to be dangerous for their interest, spread the rumor that the Republic was in danger. They fooled countless people, as in our time. Caesar Augustus fell under their blows right in the Senate. And his wife, they say, warned him after a dream she had. Better, a soothsayer supposedly even counseled him to beware of the Ides of March. This emperor differed strongly from ours who waste enormous sums of money to assure themselves a place in history. Nevertheless, the fact of talking about dreams and soothsayers makes this people more like ours.

This Roman emperor did what an African potentate has never done and will never do. This man, falling under the dagger of those whom he defended, bequeathed his gardens and three hundred sestertia per man to the people. A unique example in history according to what certain people tell me.

The singer raised his voice and some people in a neighboring room began to dance. This was not a dance, but something indefinable. A man getting up went to bow in front of a woman; she in turn stood up and the two of them, pressed against each other, turned about, while whispering sweet nothings in each other's ear. People were drinking in a corner, chatting without paying any attention to those who were dancing. This was an eye-opener for me. Here each person dances for himself, for his pleasure, while at home dancing is a collective act; the man or woman who dances does it to entertain the community when it's a secular dance, or to thank the gods in the contrary case.

Fetishism in this country is displayed ostentatiously in the streets. That had to happen since they refused to let God understand any prayers in "patois." And their audacity in this domain is such that at the entrance to the bridge leading to Flamina Nova Street, on each side, a statue of a wolf suckling two gluttonous human babies stands watch. How can anyone, when they are born under such auspices, remain temperate? Does the wolf's milk have the calming virtues of a mother's? It appears that every Roman, by some strange phenomenon, has on his tongue the very special taste of the milk his ancestors drank. That explains in part the attitude of the men here. Each one knows that he can be chosen, at any given moment in his existence, by his gods for higher services. Therefore all of them seem to have an indefinable lack of concern. They seem to be waiting for this hour marked on the clock of time. And to pass the time while waiting, they sing and dance.

In the middle of the bridge, two war-like eagles, with their wings spread, seem ready to take flight. All these gods are terribly worn by the weather. No matter, the Romans still consult them. These eagles are waiting for some mysterious signal to fly off. They have forgotten that they're old. When one is born an eagle, one remains one, one proves it even at death's door. And these eagles, their eyes fixed upon an indefinable objective, are waiting impatiently to swoop down upon some new prey. How could this old Roman people feel tired when these war-like gods invite it to a glorious destiny? Who, in the long run, would resist their call, who wouldn't like to die for his fatherland, shed his blood to water the soil of his ancestors? Has an eagle ever been vanquished? The generals are so accustomed to winning victories, to carrying home huge booties in the folds of their flags, that they have been named war eagles, if I'm not mistaken.

Conversation is difficult with these barbarians who don't understand a solitary word of my language. It was up to me to make the effort to grasp what they express with a stupifying volubility.

In short, Rome, which carried arms, fire, blood and tears everywhere, and destroyed others' beliefs, could only have a glorious history.

The two small gluttons who nurse without breathing, as if they had bet they would empty the mother wolf, were named Remus and Romulus. Two twins. Can you imagine the marvelous legend used to explain a city's origin? Do we proceed otherwise for our own? Aren't we a little Roman in this regard? But our gods aren't exposed along the streets.

In these cold countries fire plays a primary role. They liken it to a gaze or to the breath of a god.

One of the women who watched over the sacred fire, a certain Rhea Silvia, lingering at the fountain, because night fell extraordinarily fast that night, was seduced by a god of war. Ah! these men of war with their sensitive hearts and weak flesh, even when they take the form of a god! Happy time when gods mixed with men and appreciated the charms of women, and women the power of the gods. You don't really know, of gods and women, which are the stronger. This is a subject about which Roman women keep their lips sealed. They take on startled airs as soon as the conversation comes around to this subject; they pass it off with an outburst of laughter, or better yet, agreeing to talk, they gaze upon a kind of Roman scale as if to say "that depends"...Women of exceptional intelligence! And whom I suspect of very skillfully leading their husbands by the nose. Since Rhea's adventure, the gods no longer seem to appreciate the charms of women from our planet, because the adventure doesn't seem to have been repeated. Are they satiated by them? Don't they find them to their taste anymore? How you would like to ask them to really open their eyes! But they wouldn't like the makeup! heads of hair with artificial colors. So we can no longer understand each other because no woman will agree to show herself as she really is. To conquer men, doesn't woman have to try to be as beautiful as a goddess, and don't the gods take on human appearances in order to mix with us? So who will fool whom? Still, flashes of brilliance, fallen from the eyes of these divinities during the traditional small talk from which revels and tender friendships were born, have remained in the gaze of certain Roman women.

They have retained a communicative warmth, which one can judge by the liveliness of the walk, the willingness to parade, and that cheerful appearance which testifies that the Roman woman clings to life with all her might.

The war god, tired of the clash of weapons and the death rattle of the dying, was so regular at the meetings during those days when night always fell extraordinarily early, that Rhea became pregnant. The old Romans, educated according to norms that were outdated for the gods, cried scandal, not grasping the full significance of the honor which had been done them. They most certainly worshipped the gods, they offered them libations, they were prepared to leave them their last crumb of bread in order to stay in their good graces, but they obstinately refused to let any of the gods, whatever his rank, seduce the virgins charged with watching over the sacred fire. If in these moments the fire started to die, wouldn't the same gods, for fear of the cold, leave their earthly home?

There was no longer any point in having a heaven and an earth if the gods were going to come down to compete unfairly with men for the women. Unjustifiable abuse of power. The Romans saw red. The eagle was impatient to take flight. But can anyone struggle against a god? Can anyone kill the mistress of a god, the child of a god? The old Romans being very troubled, scratched their heads, some dipped snuff, others smoked. All of them thought it over. Ah, how complicated life becomes as soon as the gods stick their noses in human affairs, especially in those which precisely create the most trouble for men.

They remembered an almost analogous episode with a neighboring people, the Greeks. Danae, having given birth to Perseus, Acrisius, king of Argos, who according to the Delphi oracle was to die at the hands of one of his grandsons, had the mother and child locked in a basket, which he entrusted to the waves.

So the Romans put Rhea's twins in a wicker basket, which they pushed into the Tiber's current.

And these people thought they were shrewd? How could they not bring down the wrath of heaven when the children of a god were treated in such a way?

What prayer could be answered in the future? The wicker basket followed its destiny. The gods being one under the heavens, the wicker vessel, carefully guided by the thousand hands of the Tiber, came to rest before the shepherd Faustulus whom the gods had directed there to water his herd. He gathered up Remus and Romulus. He made herders out of them. As descendants of a war god, they were very vigorous. The contrary would have been astonishing.

After the embarkment of the twins, the old Romans waited for reprisals. They didn't come. Had the gods sanctioned their act? Were they preparing more insidious blows? Time passed. Still nothing. What was there to fear when the gods were incapable of stirring? Who in the future could prevent the Roman from parading his eagles over the face of the earth? A foolish boldness took hold of the entire race. The old Parisian, whom this boldness had won over in the early days, went about shouting from the roof tops, as if to plant panic: "What we fear is that the heaven will fall on our heads." And since the intimidated heaven stayed so quietly in its place the Parisians believed that the gods had designated them to take over for the Romans, and that they should in turn parade their rooster through every continent. The peregrinations didn't frighten the gallic rooster who is still in the best of health. Perched upon the globe,[19] he seemed to be waiting for homage from the rising sun.

Now I understand the old rabbi's proud smile as he left the plane. How could anyone unselfishly serve the child of another god when he has sent off the twins of his own gods in a wicker basket? The enigmatic smile of this man who doesn't like to share his cakes and water takes on meaning when one advances in one's knowledge of Roman history. I'm still on the periphery of it. This is to say that the harvest is going to be beautiful. What should be underlined is the weakness that the gods here have for the guardians of animals, these beings who are so close to nature and who function as they did upon leaving the factory of creation, with no added parts or habits to falsify their rhythm. On this point, Paris has very faithfully walked in Rome's footsteps. If my memory serves me right, she even seems to have left Rome far behind in these contacts. *Fluctuat nec mergitur!*[20] Why not! since a god always comes to offer his services in the most critical moments! How can anyone lose when one has such celestial trump cards in his hand? What couldn't you dare to do? And that is why Paris, Rome's godchild, seems so capricious, so lavish to an inexperienced man. Versailles, the Louvre, the Elysée, the chateaux of the Loire and other lavish residences, have been so constructed that the gods will come there to play, to mix with men and inspire the government and even business. So that the children won't divulge the secrets, you talk to them about a Santa Claus who once a year comes down the chimney to bring toys. Once the Santa Claus principle is admitted, one can easily talk with the gods during their visits. And these men think they are different from us. Why don't they get out of their hamlets, their villages? Why don't they come to our home to judge the flourishing state of affairs, the good health of our populations and hear some of our marvelous legends?

The feats of the two young herders fill several volumes, which the Roman children suckle along with the maternal milk. As adults, they no longer really know whether or not they are themselves Remus or Romulus. What boldness can't you have when you know you are a descendant of Venus, Mars and so many other gods whose daily presence is felt in the streams, the words, the wind, the flowers, the clouds, the earth? And even in the fire beside which you warm yourself every morning and every evening?

Remus and Romulus, miraculously saved from certain death, maternally brooded over and nursed by a wolf, then adopted and raised under the protection of Faustulus, the shepherd, ended up by no longer understanding each other. Men no longer know for what reasons. They don't even know whether the wolf or Faustulus saw Rhea's children first. Some maintain that the wolf was the first to see them, others that the shepherd, after having saved them, put them in the care of the wolf who agreed to nurture them. Memory has failed just as in our legends. And what is to be thought of this friendly understanding between shepherd and wolf, man and animal? The wolf nursed Remus and Romulus! What Roman woman would be willing to nurse a baby wolf? Other than from a baby bottle, of course! Exposed to the elements, the wolf continues to suckle placidly her two adoptive children without even glancing at the anonymous crowd that fills the bridges. Nothing distracts her. She knows men too well since she has been frequenting them, and the Romans in particular who believe they have done everything for her by making her a national symbol. She knows she is from the past and that today the past is in the attic. She is done a favor in being allowed to watch and grow old on a bridge in the company of two tired eagles.

Romulus' huge shadow has totally hidden Remus. Little is even known of what became of Remus. History respects only those who block up the horizon. The others she is determined to ignore. She is therefore sometimes hard to digest for the young schoolboy who prefers to gorge himself with appealing tidbits rather than with names from far away ages.

Romulus chose a valley with seven hills to found the city which has his name, Rome. Can one be astonished, with such an origin, that Rome is warlike in temperament and cannot charitably turn the other cheek as her religion recommends? If she accepted an insult, if she didn't bathe it in blood, she would offend the gods and draw their anger.

This name Rome calls to mind the many small villages back home which are named after their founder. Rome, situated at a crossroad, grew very rapidly. That's the advantage of being born under a good star. In this city of traders all beliefs rubbed elbows and were polished...Eloquence, having been cultivated, declared: "Qui langue a, à Rome va."[21] So it's not so surprising that the Romans are so verbose. And to reproach them for it indicates a total misunderstanding of their origin and history. But can you judge a people with the superficiality of a tourist after having lived among them for a long time? Am I not in the process of playing the tourist by trying to judge the Romans from first contact?

If the patience of the gods is long, their anger on the other hand is quick. Did Romulus forget that? Had he overstepped some limit? And Romulus, they say, one day disappeared, carried off by a cloud. The people, who began to wake up from their torpor, found the courage to accuse the senators of having killed him. Who at home would have such nerve? Would our people dare to raise their voice in similar circumstances? It must be recognized that the Roman people know how to shake off the yoke. How many others, gorged with misery, slowly die without even being able to complain? Roaming and hungry dogs, vehicle sirens now shoo them away from the imperial roads so that the feast cannot be interrupted. The people maintained their accusation so firmly that the Senate, in order to exonerate itself, called one of Romulus' friends who recounted: "In the course of a dream, I saw Romulus among the gods who had sent him to found the world's largest city...(in those times). The god Quirinus asks all Romans to be just, disciplined, law-abiding, and respectful toward their leaders, but terrible toward their enemies." Pathetic people, capable of being amused, appeased and contented by trifles. This force was good enough for them and like well-behaved children they went back to their chains. What had happened to the Roman blood? How one would like to know if the gods of Romulus' time, caste gods, regional gods, household gods with human rages, really placed themselves at the head of their men to wage war on their adversaries! Did they take captives? Did they leave them to their earthly generals to cultivate the land submissively?

The Romans, to my great surprise, no longer like to talk about this old story. Are they saturated with glory? Are they taking a rest? Are they ashamed that their illustrious ancestors agreed to put up with odious burdens to please problematic gods? Have they finally realized that they were taken in for so long and have for too long *marché pour des prunes*,[22] as the Parisians say? Ah, the good Roman people, just as good and just as sweet as the bread they serve you at the table! They could only attract the starving and the adventurous in quest of a place in history and a statue on a public square. So in order to get back into the good graces of Romulus-Quirinus, the people, credulous like all peoples, were respectful toward their leaders and terrible toward their enemies. Romulus was taken away by a cloud, the legend says, Did he come back to earth? Did he enter his body? Did the gods quarrel with him? Did he try to civilize them in accordance with the Roman style? The absence of information is complete on these points. Is it because of these contradictions in their history that young Romans separate themselves from it? Now they want to think by themselves. Relying upon august representatives cost them too dearly because, out of blindness or out of interest or complacency, the events under their direction too often took a particular turn. When the cooking pot was put on the common table either there was no meat, or the sauce had been eaten. As for the fried food, always salty and peppery. Judging that they were near death, the elders intended to make provisions. As if you didn't see young people die every day. The death of a young person hardly affects the old: that's Death's business and they are accorded a breather...

A guide in the forum, certainly an enemy of Rome, or one of those

Christians who never knows how to play the game, still shows "Romulus' tomb" to the tourists! Destroying such a beautiful legend! What need do they satisfy in showing that Romulus existed? Reducing Rome to the level of other peoples! But in fact, isn't showing this tomb, the only one, the tomb of a god, in the middle of the forum among the debris of marble, a way of trying to prove that Rome is different from other cities? That she was predestined to be the eternal city? That she can therefore laugh at time and the petty anger of her neighbors? Let's glide over these minute contradictions which stamp all human history. The intellectuals, with that freedom of spirit which detaches them from gods and from men, dare not express themselves on this tomb's authenticity. Excavations are done everywhere, yet they never touch this place, so as to justify either the legend or history. Roman intellectuals are neither supreme court presidents or Assize Court magistrates dressed in purple robes. Let a pick-axe touch Romulus' tomb tomorrow and something will have changed, a cord will have been broken in each Roman.

How can a people rid itself of these strata, empty itself of everything that communicates a sense to life? These statues at the thoroughfares, these wolves at the entrances to bridges, these eagles, aren't they ramparts, service stations; and what about the ruinous birthday parties, for which ragged people gladly accept to burn tens of thousands of dollars in fireworks? Can young Romans reject all of this because their history has become so burdensome? What people doesn't drag its history after it as the snail drags his shell? And it is that which makes whole peoples incapable of being assimilated. They are conscious of who they are, even if for the moment the weapons they dispose of don't allow them to be persuasive because they are expressing themselves in dialects and according to criteria which are foreign to them. What can this Roman not dare when convinced that a Roman transformed into a god is in the heavens? What obstacle could stop him? Isn't he the head, arms, feet, the automaton of the gods? Doesn't he obey voices? Hasn't this absolute confidence that the Roman has in himself, this virility inherited from a war god lingering along the paths of men, made the grandeur of the fatherland and enriched the history of this people? Haven't the men and women retained a little of this lassitude, this promptitude, this capriciousness and this thirst to create, which should constitute the character of the gods who frequented their ancestors?

I haven't yet heard mention of a god of rest. They haven't discovered him yet, or at least his voice hasn't been perceived yet; if this voice exists, it must probably be in the tonality of Mercury or Mars. It is the sign that this people was a people of workers bent upon making Rome a superb city. For each person it was a joy to shout in front of everyone: "Civis Romanus sum!" I am a Roman citizen. Wherever he went, the Roman was convinced that his god Janus, a god with two faces, one looking at the day and the other at the night, walked at his side, led him by the hand, to show him the most fertile plains and the countries with precious stones! This god Janus, who never knew which face to show, held the key to the days, months, years and centuries; it was he who opened time, if it can be expressed that way, at the beginning of every year. Whence the dark years of Roman history. Delayed in some spot, the god, surprised by the dawn, showed his night face and the Roman people could cry out: "alea jacta est."[23] However, accustomed to the language of the gods, they also changed faces...or sides.

Living is not completely restful; it's the most poisonous gift that the gods have given to men. Even to the Romans. Would existence be the beautiful adventure that it is if it didn't lead into some labyrinth in which men and nations are lost?

Their history was so beautiful, but so heavy too, that men ran from all sides to help the Romans carry it. They didn't come to share it. Several of them took out citizenship papers without having been nourished on the milk of wolves. They came to learn the gods' talk, but the gods were now mute and frightened by the affluence. Wouldn't it be paradoxical that from one day to the next, you and I could become Parisians or Romans? What would the Roman eagles, the wolf, Caesar Augustus, the Tiber, the National Assembly, the Seine, and the Palace of Versailles represent for us? We would be impressed by the richness of the palace rather than by the sum of miseries it cost the Parisians. Could we ever love Rome or Paris in the same way as those who were born there? Could we, being in Rome or Paris, extend our love to everything that these cities represent? Would we feel an integral part of everything? Would we mistake ourselves for one of the links in the chain of these cities? Wouldn't we sometimes have the feeling of being on the outside no matter what position was accorded us?

What naturalized citizen, like the old Cassius, would have been able to remove the crown from Caesar Augustus' head and place it on his knees to make him understand that Rome didn't want a king? Were the guardians of yesteryear less vigilant than the present guardians? Did they venture to reason? The proof is established, brilliantly, that they accepted things less passively in Roman than in our times. Have we become creatures of individual men? Does time while refining man remove his essential qualities?

In our times a man can no longer dare write: "I'm ashamed of being a slave." What new people would take that as a motto?

Only a Roman could say, in speaking of Caesar Augustus: "Are we going to accept, we Roman citizens, to bow down in front of him with our faces in the dust?"

No! our ancestors taught us to detest tyrants and to defend freedom as the most precious of possessions. When a people has dared to brave the gods for the banal question of an impregnated virgin, it is apt to overturn everything when it has a foreboding of chains and garrets. It never was a horse to carry stirrups, a bit and a bridle. A free mare, it trots as it pleases.

94

This country has such peaceful spots that love, liberty and sometimes idleness are cultivated there. A bad example left here by all those who through the centuries have been attracted by this land's charm. These carriers of the idleness germ, seeing the Romans imitating them, accuse them of being lazy. So the proof is made that our judgments are rarely equitable.

Some people maintain that the modern Roman no longer has the boldness and the courage of his ancestors. That is hardly astonishing. He is watching his history, engaged in preserving it from pillage and termites, in labeling and classifying it. Preoccupied with this patriotic task, he hasn't felt the time pass. Meticulous keeper of public records, little by little and unknowingly, he has broken with the gods who hardly like men who chart the position while they run the ship. Since the gods don't respond to him, he has become hesitant, somewhat timid.

The Greek example of child, abandoned to the flow of the water. It's the seal of a mentality. A certain Moses was also supposed to have been abandoned to the currents of the Nile. He also had a glorious destiny. Dead at 120, no one seems to have discovered his tomb or erected a statue to him. I wouldn't bet that specialists haven't taken up the task, so important for human history, and been content to delegate it to the exploiters of wonders.

Publicity boards, fliers and announcements will undoubtedly invite us to visit Moses' tomb in the near future. Airplanes, boats, trains, cars, photographers, guides, ticket sellers, post cards, innkeepers, sword-swallowers will form the circus in which tourists will be caught up. Ah! it all makes you think of the goads used on oxen!

The switching of the animal's tail to chase them away seems to call them on. They descend upon her en masse, as if to control her.

Men from this side of the ocean who wouldn't be able to live without heroes, having found the Greek recipe, think it a national duty to enrich their pantheons. The authorities encourage this charitable work by putting women in the position to produce gods. In this huge beehive which is their society, women don't always have the role of queen, which would have enabled them to produce gods. And that is enormously injurious to the quality of the heroes. In that fact lies the essential problem.

These children are abandoned on a street corner, in a church, because the river is too far, because there was no crib, or because at the last minute one of the mother's heart strings was moved. The isolation is such that each person must devote himself to providing for his own needs. It is true that the climate is beautiful; the men too, and furthermore, they are enterprising. The streets are numerous and there are many churches. How can one not be tempted to give unto God that which is God's so that he can make heroes, which are useful to the authorities.

Here is one of the points upon which we differ from the men here. God grant that such customs never take root upon our shores. We must create a society which allows man to live and families to maintain the bonds which bind them together. Let no child ever be abandoned in our streets and our churches. Let us protect ourselves from imitations and caricatures. Let's not put our confidence in the façades of monuments; they have foundations whose importance escapes us. Oh! Rome frightens me as much as Paris! How uneasy their seductive power makes me! Are we armed for an eventual struggle? Yes, if we become aware of the foundations of what Rome and Paris call civilization. We lack heroes in the Western sense; we need not create any. Not only is their upkeep expensive, but their susceptibility grows so fast that they become pests. The new classes who gravitate around them become so arrogant that the people no longer know what burdens them more, the leaders and their entourage or daily existence. The people here are richly endowed, and the names of heroes, even on their books, still spew streams of blood. Let's protect ourselves from these marble and bronze presents, from these moulds conceived for another continent and which, under our naturally intemperate sky, would only too quickly become monstrous. The sun and the rain have a propensity for excess and everything that they touch always suffers from gigantism. It occurs to me that the men here would push us towards this route only in the hope of flooding us with products stamped with the effigy of those who would be our leaders. If I were a leader, I really wouldn't like to see my portrait on materials, perfume flasks, bus tickets and match boxes.

The Roman woman who knows her history perfectly—just like the Parisian woman—now takes care not to wear necklaces. Not only does she intend not to be bridled, but what hero could serve as her pendant? In addition, numerous are those who do not pierce their ears. This practice allows them to be deaf at will and saves them from all gaffes. And it's since they have taken to going deaf that the gods no longer visit them. And here is one of the reasons why Rome no longer produces Romuluses. Moreover, Faustulus having died without a descendant, the Tiber would refuse to be burdened with new wicker baskets. Everyone knows that here in Rome the child carries the father's name. The family is vertical. Ours, which is horizontal, is certainly burdensome in times of happiness, but how precious it is in times of misfortune. Here, the living move about in the same rooms. The dead sleep in the same house called a burial vault, which only the rich can acquire. They are looking for the solution to problems which have been resolved from the beginning in our land: helping one another because we are all of the same family, cherishing children and never mistaking ourselves either for God's gift to mankind or for a god. This attitude gives us a freedom of movement, which many people envy. To acquire it, most people spend their time burning candles. I don't know if the candle manufacturers have an understanding with men of the robe* since the quantity of candles lit in this

*They say cloth.

country seems astronomical to me. Luckily all these flames don't rise to the heavens because the risk of a fire would be great. But the gods have foreseen everything, the sky here is of a prodigious height. Even the clouds remain rather high in the sky, so much does the ardor of faith seem disquieting to them. Those which are charged with bringing rain stay on the hills and it's from there that they pour their contents upon the city. Or if by chance the order is given to push on to the middle of the city, it's with a gallop that they accomplish their mission. The clouds of Rome are holy clouds, which hardly like to get wet. They also...

The Roman's smile, uncaring and sonorous, would like to be imposing. The "Papa" is there: everytime he makes the sign of the cross, he sanctifies each citizen's life. Angels are bent over the city around which they stand guard. So the Roman, convinced of being rejected by Satan because of the holy air that he has always breathed, just like us, doesn't hurry for anything. Because of this you don't feel the dizziness here that Paris gives. The Romans don't walk in step nor do they run about on assembly lines. Undoubtedly there are factories which apply Parisian working methods. That offends the Roman so much that as soon as the departure signal sounds, he dashes outside to breathe an air that is no longer distributed by assembly line. In reaction, he walks slowly. That's why you see so many people dragging their feet in Rome. This surprises the Parisian, but after two days, he falls in step. He becomes Roman, that is to say he returns to his origins. As if to wash him of all his Parisian contaminations, they try to show him the "Papa." Isn't he the lost sheep who is coming back to the fold? Does anyone know what germs he brings, the ideas that are fermenting in his head? Since Julius Caesar – that was Caesar Augustus' first mate – the Parisians have sometimes had questionable reactions, which prove that they weren't able to digest Roman values. Thus, it is a godsend when some of these people, under the guise of vacations, wedding trips, honeymoons, etc., came back on a pilgrimage to the source of their culture. The Parisian who has been told by all the manuals that time is money, that he must know how to make use of it, that he mustn't waste it, is very shocked to see the Roman waiting for him on a cafe terrace or on a garden bench. Thus the awareness grows inside him. He discovers the most terrible of frauds: that men have cut time up for him into hours, minutes and seconds. He understands why he wears a number in the factory. At the entrance, he leaves his personality behind and plays a role. Does he really have to think to tighten a bolt? Who wouldn't throw away a tool if he had to think? Just as discipline makes the strength of armies, automation makes that of factories. Because factories proliferate wars, each product is a bullet, a soldier. The waves of wars which descend upon men are but floods from factories. It is enough to open a valve with a purpose. The Parisian discovers all of this in his contact with Rome. But too Parisian to be a deserter, he will return to his factory like a brave soldier programmed to walk in step. Walking in step is one of the principal strengths of the people here. It's the only opportunity offered them to live in community. The sound of one person's steps encourages the steps of the other. So they join hands as they march toward death but divide up at dinner time. Singing heartily as if to frighten the enemy they form columns, pushing one another and with no one permitted to look behind. At least sheep leave the herd. Nothing of the sort here. Their feet become those of the centipede.[24] A herd has only one head, one tail, one body and thousands of feet. But can a foot think? And the paradox is that here men spend enormous sums to teach their children to think. Can you think when you're a foot? Puzzling; the sheep who leaves the herd has an advantage over man: he only has four feet!

* * *

Nowhere, couples kissing or in each others' arms. I only noticed the discreet gesture that a woman makes to a man that she's just leaving. On the benches, discreet lovers. How could the gods waste their time on earth, when the women show such weariness, and all of them seem so dull?

When Venus has presided at the birth of a city, it is important to put a corset on love and a garrotte on men's hearts. A holy city with one hundred and fifty-seven churches wouldn't be able to lead any other sort of existence. So it isn't in Rome that you will see a man driving a car, allowing himself to be tickled by a woman playing the kitten. Road accidents will have causes other than stealing a kiss at a bend in the road, as can happen elsewhere. Everyone, in all circumstances, remains cool, self-conscious, is on his guard, weighs his sentence, his gesture, or his look, especially when he knows that any trifle would be enough to release the phenomena that would tarnish the city's white halo. Rome is a city of high temperatures which the use of pasta doesn't succeed in lowering. But what would the Roman live on if he didn't have pasta? Vicious circle, and that's why everyone stands watch so as to limit the fires.

* * *

Over rooftops, airplanes blink that seem to be ready to land; here, it's the luminous sign of a dressmaker or an industrialist, there, the pastry cook's glowing sign. No producer wants to remain obscure. The psychology of the people from this side of the ocean is contained in these flashy signs. Just as in Paris, one must attract attention, convince and be the only master. They serve to wage war on two fronts: interior and exterior. The people are always mobilized against themselves or others. The rifle, the knife, shovel, pick-axe, and chisel are also very offensive weapons.

Eternal crusades!

Horses and dragons on public squares spit streams of water, lions vomit theirs.

Ties in all colors. One is tempted to believe that ties are the only national product. But the ardent Roman imagination lets itself run freely in a thousand other objects.

A descendant of hunters accustomed to distinguishing animals by their smell, I'm smelling the occupations of certain people from a distance, occupations which "Papa" disapproves of everyday, but what can't be allowed when one is in the terrestrial paradise? in Rome?

An exceptionally rich day! leaving Paris, reaching Rome and learning everything which precedes is proof that the gods have taken me under their protection. Taxis pass, numerous ones; streetcars too, packed. To mix with this sympathetic crowd, I get on a streetcar. The people, kindly, make room. A little too much in my opinion because the empty area around me annoys me as much as the stares that are fixed on me. Do they think I'm coated with tar? A gentleman, holding his wife by the arm, talks to me but smiles when he sees that I don't understand him. In turn, I smile, and it's only then that we understand each other.

For having helped a child off and having held up an old woman who was about to slip, all the faces look at me. No, I don't come from hell. At home gods don't burn their creatures and if I'm black, it's because I was created by a god who was tired of seeing everything in white. Try seeing everything in white yourselves, you'll get dizzy! I'm there to break the monotony. These Romans, they don't know it. The streetcar passengers are no longer surprised that I'm black but that I have the same gestures as they do: helping a child, an elderly person. Seeing me, brushing against me, the devil to whom they've given our color must seem likeable to them. And it's in this regard that we're one step ahead of these people who push possessiveness to such a degree that they never let go of their wives' arms.

We haven't made either gods or devils of them. Certainly their color seemed strange, peculiar, even a bad omen to us. Undoubtedly, the first ancestor who saw them emerging from the forest confused them with some of our spirits and ran away with his wives and children; but very quickly, he got over his fright and accepted them as men.

* * *

First night in Rome. A cold night. A night without dreams.

Ah! no, I was wrong, the Roman gods aren't with me; for them the barbarian that I am could not have understood their message. So they sent me a heavy sleep in the course of which I could even have been carried away without realizing it. If you really think about it, after such a loaded day, what else could the gods dispatch to me if not such a sleep? But would I be a man, if I were satisfied with this lot?

When I awoke, it was raining. A timid and pathetic rain bent on spoiling my morning. The hours passed slowly. Buses and cars passed, splashing water on the pedestrians. Some wore old raincoats riddled with holes into which the water tried to penetrate. A rain without thunder, or lightning, a silent rain couldn't really frighten me.

At a sign, a taxi stops on the other side of the street. At that precise moment, the rain intensifies with muffled rumblings. Could I retreat with the battle already enjoined? I put my nose out as we usually do in such cases. At home, the rain, very courteous, diminishes in violence out of respect for our nose, this extremely delicate, indispensable and even decorative organ. The Roman rain, most certainly curious or mischievous, was revoltingly impolite. It made a real drum out of my nose. My nostrils, revolted, spread with rage. Such a revolt having never been seen in Rome before, the rain got offended: black nostrils flaring under a caress! Come on! At that precise moment, another little burst of thunder. War was declared. I held out the back of my right hand, she beat it violently. How I wanted to laugh and tell her: "Eh, honey, at home, when the rain falls with all its strength, when the thunder cries out from the depths of its lungs, children leap with their feet joined together in the water to play. So to intimidate me, you would have to get up pretty early in the morning." A very violent burst of thunder made me jump. Having understood me, had the gods given a warning shot to the rain? The water that streamed down penetrated under the awning where I was.

Romans remained attentive to my moves while pretending to be discussing among themselves. Must the retreat be sounded? I would have done it if a woman hadn't offered me a place next to her under her umbrella. It is the first time since I left our country that an unknown woman has done such a thing for me.

Rome has spontaneous acts. It was enough that I was a man and beaten by the rain for this woman to reawaken to the feelings of the vestal virgin charged with keeping alive the fire of friendship.

I forgot that it was raining.

How can one not linger near women of this type especially when one is a god of war? How can one not like Rome where charming gazes, delicate gestures and eternally youthful attitudes are allied with a mild climate?

A cold wind blows without stopping as if giving all its meaning to the word "home" whether it be the hearth or the family. Alone, I feel the cold more. I have dry, cracked, white skin. We weren't made for these climates. I'm no longer astonished by the preeminent role of the virgins and I understand why the Romans buried them alive, if by weariness or negligence, they let the fire which warmed the gods die out.

Tourist buses follow upon one another, each one carrying its country's insignia. Wandering people, the men from these ocean shores have retained the habit of running around the world to satisfy their curiosity. Distributing their own memory, in shoulder bags they drag cameras and papers along with them, which help them untangle the spindle of memories. The Romans watch them placidly as they pass.

All the vehicles go at breakneck speed. At every moment you expect an accident that doesn't happen. The drivers turn without slowing down and stop without warning. Always without difficulty. And at the same time they have such courtesy and gallantry! I've seen some of them stop at a green light to let a pedestrian cross, to allow a woman to pick up her handkerchief or a child to join his parent on the other side of the street. A paradise for pedestrians. The authorities have succeeded in bridling the destructive instinct which reigns in the hearts of those behind the wheel.

Rome is in better health for it and remains a human city, a city of poets who don't let themselves be dominated either by machines or by tall houses. A well-balanced city. Philosophical people. The Roman amusingly observes the new laurel gatherers and lets each one meditate upon the ruins of his monuments. Charitably, he likes to share his experience. He remembers a certain Brennus, who, leading his troops, came to stir up trouble for a moment in the city, at the hour when the gods "were napping" on the capitol. This Brennus believed himself victorious and throwing his sword on a scale shouted: "Misfortune to the vanquished!" That really meant: "Give me all of your gold." This statement so impressed the Romans that they became Brennus' disciples. Indiscretions of youth. Since then, they have grown and matured, and even if they no longer consult augurs, they remain authentic Romans, that is to say men who really know what they want and who will put in the time needed to attain a goal. They watch the flood of tourists pass by, these modern vandals who ransack landscapes and masterpieces. These nomads note that in Rome, the square has softened its severity and that curved lines abound.

The Roman doesn't imitate. He studies other techniques to better express what is unique in him. The buildings are different, each flower has its indolent way of climbing balconies or falling down from them. The colors burst forth in harmonious marriage, while on a street corner an illuminated Madonna stands watch. Roman faith flows over with love. Does the Roman have a lot to be forgiven for? Is that why the "Papa" spends nights praying?

Carnivorous people whose history is made up of blood and bodies, just like their neighbors who all have the pages of blood in their book of gold...

Red light. Stop. The signals all suspended across the street.

Gas stations, the same as in Paris: Esso, Mobil, Energol. A democratic coalition of interests which tends to bend the people under the same law. But Rome wouldn't be able to admit that new values could be trampled underfoot since they serve as a standard during troubled periods. The Pope watches over them, the father of all Christian nations. The Pope is too human to be just Roman; and he is too Roman to be universal.

Men here like to go to the heart... of things. And if they talk with their arms, it's to shove aside those who don't understand.

"Bevetti Coca-Cola" recommend the signs in front of the cafés and at certain corners. The same command is given in Paris: "Buvez Coca-Cola." To consume the same beverage is to acquire the same modes of thought. Men here are so convinced of the power of what we call "the satisfaction of the stomach" that everything begins or ends with libations which they call cocktails in which champagne and Coca-Cola are included. So Coca-Cola, very calmly, ushers in a younger, more dynamic, more twentieth-century culture. It unites continents which march briskly toward the "Coca-Cola civilization." The representatives of this new civilization are so discreet that they don't try to occupy any key posts. They seem to follow everything from afar, through field glasses. What's important is the consumption of Coca-Cola, and it's not by showing off that they can assure it. On the contrary, Roman susceptibility and distrust are such that diplomacy must be used.

What makes the Coca-Cola representatives despair is their height. They are noticeable from far down the street. Their discretion becomes unwieldy at certain moments as they bring out their latest formula without trumpets and drums, as if in playing, just to give it some air.

The Coca-Cola civilization has neither the wild boar, the wolf, the elephant, nor even the eagle or the vulture in its arsenal. It's undoubtedly such novelty that is responsible for its popularity with the Romans.

If Paris demands an effort to get to know her great men, Rome, on the other hand, spares you all fatigue. Each street sign indicates that X, born in ... died in..., was a good engineer, poet, general or condottiere cardinal. The foreigner lives Roman history more than he does Paris'. Rome is a book open to the wind.

Let's not be ashamed of wearing panther skin across our chests, crocodile-teeth necklaces or eagle feathers in our hair. That is ascribable more to coquettishness than to culture, because I have just seen Roman soldiers with feathers in their hats and crossed bones on their arms. They tell me that there was a time when tibias supported a skull. That was simply to show that the batallion that wore this insignia showed no mercy to victims. And these soldiers are followed by wives with short, black hair dragging behind them three or four children who hold each other's hand. Do these women walk in the footsteps of their ancestor who, to a friend asking her to show her jewels, presented her two sons?

Do they march to improve their figures? The Roman figure with time and alluvium seems singularly solid. So I haven't met any of the mason wasps you see so often in Paris. Certainly the women wear belts but they don't transform them into garottes.

* * *

The Capitol of Campidoglio, in the indigenous dialect, is the most venerable of the hills surrounding Rome. The king of the Roman gods, Jupiter Capitolin, lived at its summit. The old Rome, obsessed with peace, was surrounded by an eleven kilometer wall with sixteen gates. This wall is still erect. In case of hostilities, the men hurriedly regained the city whose doors were closed. If by chance the doors remained open, the city was declared open and the laws of war prohibited violence and looting. These organized people had foreseen everything. A people conscious of their own values.

With time, undoubtedly to provide work for the relatives of some Emperor, the number of gates grew. Four were reserved for the city's most important saints, Giovanni, Pancrazio, Paolo and Sebastiano. In this apportionment the Holy Spirit wasn't forgotten. There is a "Via Santo Spirito'" which probably leads to the establishment with the same name. I wasn't able to investigate this last fact because the usually verbose Romans show a somewhat awkward reserve everytime we broach this subject. The spirit no longer breathed in them. Like us they have subjects that they don't like to discuss in public. However, God knows I am as Roman as they are. Do they doubt my conversion? Do they think that the undercurrents deep inside will one day rise up within me to wash away what they have offered? Ah! I understood. My name hasn't been Romanized. It should have ended in I, O, or A. But it has remained pagan, rebellious to every command. Rome would have welcomed me with wide-opened arms if I had had a poetic name or if I had been one of its Angels with a Golden Mouth! My mouth has remained the one that mixes up prayers. And my feet still aren't accustomed to her dances. Rome would certainly like me to contribute something new. And I show up only under the guise of a consumer. Now if there are so many gates to the city, it's because it is open to all influences. I'm a looter. And Rome prizes men of my type.

Make myself Roman! Is it possible? We can say the same prayers to the same God but to give up my own skin, to wear another face or acquire a new attitude seems very improbable. And Rome being aware of it detains me on the threshold.

A wide staircase leads to the Capitol where a crowd of tourists mills about. Two statues, each one representing a man holding the reins of a reared-up horse, welcome the visitors. These are the dioscuri Castor and Pollux, probably the ancient guardians of the sacred hill. Like palace guards. Today we would say "bodyguards." Their stare, lost in the distance, testifies that they are also watching over Rome, ready to mount their mares to throw out all the city's enemies. The coming and going, the noise made by tourists, the cries of children, leave them indifferent. These are domestic noises, noises of admirers. And so they don't move, not for a single moment.

In the center of the square, the equestrian statue of a king or of a god. It's the same thing. Besides, States are returning to their ancient tradition of turning men into gods, erecting statues to them and giving their names to bridges, squares, sections of cities and villages. Out of gratitude, they say. Obviously, what wouldn't you do for a being who proposed to extol you?[25] And the modesty of the new gods is such that they never refuse any of these signs of gratitude. That encourages them in the chosen path. The gods are so made that they don't always understand men. They don't understand that men, through fear, yield to them the nourishment that they need.

In an old room full of gossipers, a powerful white, marble statue with an enormous base. Here, a hand, the index pointed toward the sky, there, a headless body, a bodiless head, scattered limbs. These are supposedly the cut up remains of a king named Constantine.

Lying down or erect, these statues attest to the grandeur of an epoch, to the prodigious dream of the Romans, and preach humility.

The universe is too vast for us to fill it with our activity alone.

We occupy only an insignificant part of the stage and we fade away at our own speed. Submerged, we clutch everything to ourselves to stay afloat. So everyone possesses his god, his spirits and his sun. The old Roman people haven't escaped this disease for they speak of their heaven.

These statues! debris of creation that one would have wanted to be permanent and which time disjoints! They were asked to magnify a reign, a history, to be its heralds. There they are crumbling into dust.

Do statues and civilizations walk together?

When you contemplate these statues, you wonder how those who created them lived. They used wood furniture and clay or wooden plates. Everything resided in their hearts. No tyrant could prevent the dreams of a man who had said everything when he had declared simply: "Civis Romanus sum!" Nations come here to read by Roman light. That is so true that the Parisian artist has no status until he has sojourned among the Roman statues. Difficult test, for these witnesses of man's progress never surrender their secrets. Their muteness is irritating. It constitutes their power. Men err in studying them. Their truth is in their silence.

To the right of the capitol is the Tarpeian rock. The Romans got rid of traitors and covetous men by throwing them off its summits. So Rome teaches temperance and balance.

If the Romans increased the number of doors to the city, it's because with time their blood became hotter and they had to have movement and space. The first warm-blooded animal was the Roman, according to the Parisian. An appraisal that hardly respects the Roman, who at certain moments begins to wonder if he should continue to consider the Parisian simply as a cousin, or as a first cousin, since he is sometimes so belligerent. The people here are all united by family ties. They deny it, just to deceive the foreigner and put him on. Their wars are family quarrels waged to reclaim a jewel left by an ancestor. But they take such proportions that each time you would think the end of the world was approaching. No one knows exactly what happens: the day after these disasters, men come out from everywhere, more numerous still than before the battle. And they line up crosses in the cemeteries. These are people who don't like to be dry-eyed and whom I suspect... I must be careful on this last point. They have so many tricks!

The latest fashion is to dress in imitation panther or camouflage material. The mentality of camouflage grows with time. And it's disturbing when you know the morbid taste they have here for power.

One day, the Romans, adventurers who came from all over to found the city, being without wives, organized a feast to which they invited the young girls from the surrounding area. They watched them dance and the more they danced, the desire grew in them to have women. And the young girls must not have done anything to cool the Roman ardor. So they were carried off. As a result of this abduction a war broke out between Rome and her neighbors. A long, exhausting, indecisive war.

One's Honor is washed in blood. A sovereign contempt of human life.

One day the Sabin king, Tatius, on a reconnaissance mission, met a young Roman girl wearing a large quantity of jewels, at the fountain. Her name was Tarpeia. The enemy king promised her heaps of gold jewelry if she helped him get into the citadel. She agreed. And thus the Sabins, one night, succeeded in marching to the Capitol where the Romans had retired under Jupiter Capitolin's watch. The Sabins are people of their word. Each one came with a gold bracelet. When passing in front of Tarpeia, they threw it in her face. So she died under a pile of gold, the young girl who liked gold too much.

Some geese ended up saving the Romans, who, out of gratitude, consume them on every menu.

Tarpeia! Mansilus! and others still! Gold's malefic power has been known since the height of antiquity and it was undoubtedly to reduce its effect that one of the Three Wise Men had the ridiculous idea of bringing gold to Jesus Christ. So gold was exorcised. And in order that it never fall under the devil's influence again, it is housed in the Bank of the Holy Spirit.

Time passed with its pageantries and parades. Rome was drunk with history... Today, on the sinister square, the Tarpeian Rock where the spirits of traitors groaned, magnificent gardens flourish in whose paths children play and tourists rest. A young girl is reading. A telephone rings in one of the offices at the place. Down below, workers armed with electric drills redo a street. Buses pass crammed with foreigners.

Taking a short cut paved with large black stones between which grass pushes up, I arrive at the ancient village square. An accumulation of debris and of history torn by time: the pride of men conquered by bad weather. The tall marble columns struck down by the anger of the gods. Religious celebrations and political meetings took place at the Forum. The spirit of trade is pushed to such a point that in order to visit this cemetery, you have to pay a tax. So I go to get in line when I hear someone running towards me. I stop, turn around, and who is approaching me?... the Roman gods have such delicacies. A ravishing young girl dispatched finally to welcome me and to make me better appreciate the beautiful colors of the Roman sky, which I had begun to find grey. I admit it was about time. Giving me a bed with two pillows and sending me a deep sleep constituted a true abuse of power. At any rate, better late than never, says one proverb. My nervous heart had already panicked, it did somersaults, in spite of my wise counsel of prudence. Obviously when you don't understand a language, you never know what vessel you're embarking upon when a woman approaches you. The heart isn't a good companion in such cases. Unsophisticated, and a rebel to all modernism, mine only thinks of doing things its own way, even in Rome where you have to know how to navigate among the gods, the dead and the living. An African heart that knows what it is and what it represents in this world of born diplomats and experienced swimmers. The Roman gods, accustomed to intermingling with men to laugh at their expense, sent me a messenger who couldn't understand me. A dialogue of deaf-mutes was opened; it would be better to say a dialogue of smiles. She swung her hips and batted her eyelashes to punctuate her sentences, flipped through her English book. Her black eyes had eloquent reflections. When you are Roman, you can't help but be voluble when near the Forum. As for myself, I didn't know what to answer. My smile seemed pretty lame next to my interlocutor's musical volubility. I finally understood that she was appealing to my kindness for a charitable work. Obviously when you are in Rome you can't help but sympathize with all suffering. Barely had I given her my donation than she set out in pursuit of other passersby, after having gratified me with a very sweet "gratiae". I watched her leave. Could I do otherwise? The gods continued to treat me like a barbarian. I found them uncivil and primitive; gods who could no longer read in men's hearts! How could they help the Romans to understand other men? And I looked at the ruins I was about to desecrate! the forum which I was going to tread! Certainly, we don't speak the same language, but must the gods discriminate?

They are there, in ruins, the temples into which thousands of faithful squeezed and the triumphal arches under which legionaries passed. The Temples of Saturn, Vesta, Antonin and Faustine, the arch of Septimus Sevres, weather has respected nothing. Here human vanity bursts forth.

Here men have sung, danced, laughed and cried, men convinced that the world ended with them.

A cat slips through the grass; birds perch here and there, workers sing while repairing a triumphal arch. It's the Concord Temple erected to commemorate the peace between Patricians and Plebians, the two classes of the society of the day. On this square, the voice of Cicero, the most famous of their orators, rang out.

"For how long, Catalina, will you abuse our patience? How long will your madness mock us?"

This Catalina was a young man who, attacking the Senate and Cicero, the rich people's man, denounced the injustices of the powerful and called upon the weak to unite for a revolution. Cicero wanted his adversary declared a public enemy. The Senators didn't go along with Cicero in the brutal decision he desired. Old Rome proved to be democratic. The word "dictatorship" which in our day parades proudly on every street corner, undoubtedly hadn't yet seen the light of day. And anyone could live with the inconsistencies, just like at home.

The wind of public opinion shifts fast. Cicero, the great champion of justice, the rich people's man, was assassinated one day. This still happens in our day and age. The people, satiated with lies and miseries, shrug their shoulders and rid themselves of a bothersome man.

Was this a warning for those who, like Verrès, prided themselves in having divided their wealth into three parts: "one for themselves, one for the judges, one for the lawyers?"

It seems that modern heads of state and their acolytes have found a new way to save their fortunes from the angry masses. They place it in a mountainous and inaccessible country which some people call Switzerland. The neuralgic center of gold, so neuralgic that she stays out of all the wars which she keeps up and nourishes. And the great war powers break loose and lose their heads in vain; they will never succeed in unleashing strife upon this chosen soil of the god, Gold.

Rome was to be shaken by the name of Spartacus. Spartacus, slave in revolt, levied a troop and hid in the mountains; today they would call him a guerrilla. A good general, he defied and disregarded all of the Roman magistrates dispatched against him, took away their emblems and their treasure. What? A slave accomplishing such stunning feats? A slave conquering Patricians? What were the gods doing? Were they now siding with the mob?

What would become of the world if the people were to play a primary role? Didn't they risk sweeping aside the privileged minority?...

Here the voice of another orator, the Old Cato, rang out. And that other emperor, Nero, adorned with an incendiary halo! He reigned long after the birth of the Jesus Christ the rabbi's ancestors had not been expecting.

This child of God came, certainly, but in distressing simplicity, as if to begin his mission from the very first. And what is worse, in a stable, preferring the company of animals to that of men. In the real world, does a god without silver and parchment have the freedom of the city? So he was rejected. What kind of attitude would we have adopted under the circumstances?

Preaching reconciliation among divided tribes, among men, people and nations, he acquired great popularity among the working classes, among those who, to merit paradise, must give the little that they have to God, as if the Creator had to live on charity coming from trembling hands and distressed hearts. Jesus fought against the notion of such a God.

"Love one another," he didn't cease to proclaim. A difficult test for beings accustomed to considering others only in relation to what they could get from them, from their naiveté, their blood or their greed.

To accept that no one suffer from hunger, cold or breach of trust, that no one be robbed, beaten, ransacked or chained, that no state, no nation could be enslaved? That was spreading revolution. Could an authentic child of God upset the old order of things? What would the new elements of power be without weapons and wealth?

Who could one love when God himself took pleasure in multiplying the colors and the shapes of heads and in diversifying languages?

What did the Wise Men from the East say to this Jesus? What did he confide to these augurs who saw his star in the East? Peter spoke of his Master who loved humble people, of the coming of a more brotherly world, of a world in which men will have the courage to look each other in the face, to think of their neighbor's hunger and thirst.

Everything in Rome is current in spite of the centuries. Nero had a philosopher named Seneca as his mentor. He profited so much from the lessons of this illustrious Master that he abolished indirect taxes, notably reduced payments to informers in the hope of discouraging them from bringing accusations against the discontent.

In our time, not only are they paid generously and given precedence over honest men, but their numbers are being increased. They are the pillars of modern societies. A new class of civil servants.

This Seneca must have been one of our men lost on this side of the globe. Speaking like our elders, he repeated to his student what our parents say to us: "It's not beauty that should please a husband in his wife, it's her honor, fidelity and modesty. These are the only things that last; each passing day deflowers beauty..." Not satisfied to think like us, he allowed himself to fulminate against slavery, which constituted the foundation of Roman society. Obviously, accused of being bad citizens, the philosophers, who weren't always docile griots, were not liked. They all had either to open their veins or drink hemlock.

A philosopher is too conscious of who he is and of what he represents to play the puppet. All of these events and many more have had these broken marble columns, this cratered earth and these basilicas in ruins as their backgrounds. From the basilicas, the prayers must certainly have no longer risen toward the gods. Was this to mark the end of an era? to say that they preferred churches built in joy to those constructed in tears, hardship and by force?

Eloquent ruins of basilicas and temples! The gods don't want people to bring them sighs only, but also and especially happy dreams, they want people to talk to them without trembling and not to come to them in their temple to ask for a place in heaven! Heaven is not won by deserting the earth.

No! the world wasn't created either in suffering or in blood but in harmony and peace. The people here seem to be oblivious to that. Each one wants to find his salvation, forgetting that he is bound to others and responsible for others.

What the gods want is the show we put on in coming together in this old Rome, in smiling at each other, in mutually yielding our places with courtesy, without even knowing our last names, first names and positions!

* * *

After having marched her eagles through several climates, Rome, now returned to her bed, in order to digest in peace, changes tactics and proposes a new language to the world. She will no longer go to other peoples, but will ask them to flock toward her, to make an effort to understand her and to walk at her sides. She will cover them with her shadow, with her flags and with her history. She will share all of her wealth with them and will, in addition, give them illustrious heroes so no one will feel either out of place or deprived.

When Saint Peter shoots his arrows so high into the sky, it's so as to be seen from afar, and to play the role of a beacon in the night of consciousness.

Certain of being in possession of the key to the door of heaven watched over by guardians understanding only Latin – the only dialect that Saint Peter was able to teach them – Rome opens her arms to us all and in so doing gives us access to paradise.

Since men are not aware enough of their own worth, Rome wants to free them from their caverns, even though they be skyscrapers, from their ruts and their chains. She wants to erect a bridge over skin colors and mountains uniting men by disciplining stomachs, by teaching stomachs to march in step, nerves to have the same reactions and nostrils to palpitate at the smell of the same meals. Men eating in the same way very quickly dress the same way, and even more quickly join hands and dance while singing the same song.

* * *

"Felici faustoque ingressui," "Happy and prosperous entrance," had been written upon one of her doors, the Door of the People, as if to say that her plan is to make men happy from now on. No one here will be treated as a slave or suffer injustice! Do you flee from an inhuman country? Well, Rome opens her doors to you. She presses you against her old bosom, and invites you to suckle the wolf in order to become a true citizen.

What must one renounce or admit to in order to be a Roman citizen?

The grandiose plan which Rome has conceived is the incurable illness of assimilation.

For the Latins, other peoples are there to be cut up. It follows then that if tomorrow we also were to place ourselves among Rome's followers, those who brought us these values would demand total abdication from us. At that price, when we die, we will be permitted to receive absolution and to receive the exceptional privilege of lying next to outstanding dead men in a flowered cemetery.

"Felici faustoque ingressui," with all the experiences acquired in the course of your travels, contributing to making this city, this country, the place from which the true conception of world civilization will emanate. Our statues have aroused gods' anger; our temples have given way under the curses of others of our slaves.

We don't always polish our signs to show that Rome gives little value to gold. Don't look at our banks, not even the Bank of the Holy Spirit. These are old bulwarks, which time is undermining. Mingle with our men and you will grasp all the freshness of our sentiments. Only an old people knows how to love! And we are an old people!

So enter, pilgrim, into this holy city, with everything that will permit you to be a worthy Roman citizen; a man of influence, of words, an honest man. Even if the values have changed, the principle stays the same: "Civis Romanus sum!" The door is there, without a clapper or a guard. It's enough to pass under the arch, and to show proof of alliance for Rome to welcome you.

And God only knows how good hearted we are! Our errors, the split skulls, the seized cities, were an excess of goodness. If we hug all the world to our rough bosom with some force, it's in order to give the full weight of love back to the kiss, since this greedy Judas had given it another meaning.

And if we distrust certain kisses, on the other hand, we appreciate our own most famous vintage: the Lacryma Christi. These tears nourish us and open up heavenly perspectives to us. Now do you understand why we have so many poets, singers and musicians accustomed to soaring in the clouds and stars?

* * *

Not knowing, in spite of all their studies of what man becomes after death, the Romans claim that the butterfly which flies around a flame in the evening is the soul of a dead person. Ah! how many butterflies we should find in the forum and elsewhere where this highly civilized people played with life in a strange way!

Men trained to kill each other, to the great joy of the spectators, gave free reign to their instincts in a huge edifice called the Coliseum. It had twenty-four entrances, one of which, through which the combatants penetrated, has the name "Door of Life" and the other, through which the vanquished left, "Door of Death." Once in the arena, the gladiators greeted the Emperor by saying to him: "Greetings, Caesar, those who are going to die salute you!" Making a profitable game of death for other individuals! and crowning the assassins! Is this really Roman? Isn't having them applauded by thousands of spectators, training men to despise life, their fellow man and to inculcate the taste of blood in them? So it's no longer astonishing that for them war is the spice of life. It feeds their anxieties and makes business prosper.

So the marble from the Coliseum served to build twenty-two churches and palaces. A church in Rome is a monument proportional to the people. And every fifteen minutes a mass is said. A people mobilized in prayer and devotion who sometimes feel a need to escape. A Roman is a holy man who works under the watch of Christ hung on the office wall. What harm could you do that is not already absolved or sanctified? What devil could live in this atmosphere of incense and prayer? Some Romans know that and assume a certain independence toward the Church.

This assurance of dying in an aura of holiness within the Roman walls gives a strange frankness to some men. They wouldn't want to get caught in any thorn, in any difficulty. They bend to all angles and wiggle out of all complicated situations with a pleasing smile. They have a luster, a polish which protects them from all snags. Veterans in everything. And their enemies who don't attain this suppleness in spite of centuries of imitation and continued efforts, call them talented comedians. This is hardly an insult because in countries on this side of the ocean, those who earn their living easily, who have their photograph splashed on the front pages of newspapers are comedians, especially the women when they're young, pretty and when they're in what they call the movies. New queens who have a court comprised of men from all classes. They turn the cities upside down and set in motion a world of rubbernecks, photographers, post card sellers and autograph seekers. Sometimes it's the smile, the bosom or the shape which are admired in them. Moreover, they know how to wear make-up, that is, always showing themselves in the most favorable light. These new queens don't know where to hang their hearts and journalists follow them around through binoculars. A very envious lot because many are the young girls who dream of becoming stars, *étoiles*. A people of corporations constantly in need of a master to regulate the ballet.

An old people broken down from all the feats and who constantly remain in the middle road between the devil and the Holy Spirit.

The Romans are so positive that they "operate *à la française*" only grudgingly, in the same way the French "slip away *à l'anglaise.*" And the Roman rulers have such confidence in themselves that they don't much like to stand aside, get lost or drown behind the steering wheel of long, shiny colored cars. Chosen by their compatriots, never stable, and maintained by exotic armies, these rulers move about on the stage like all actors of the world, receiving applause, insults which they never take into account, hearing threats they scorn from the heights of their Roman grandeur and when the wind turns they return to their homes with much dignity, with the same bearing as when they climbed to the Capitol. Governing is a ballet which every party is intent on dancing, so as to not remain an eternal spectator. For the foreigner, Roman life presents no backwash. Everything seems to be worked out among friends, in the family, because, being religious people in the highest sense of the word, each of them holds in horror hate, selfishness, degradation and war, so they say.

Churches don't get empty. An incessant coming and going of believers. They follow the rhythm of the factories which run night and day. We have always thought that the night was made for resting. The people on this side of the ocean think just the opposite. They exploit the night, and even more feverishly than the day. Time, they say, is money. At this rate life has become such a complex problem that they can't make head or tail of it.

Here they have an ardent desire to reach paradise for a well deserved rest. This is to say that they reject the circus their existence has become. Incapable of developing the earth, men are preparing trips to other planets. Always the itching for conquest. Undoubtedly they would like to export to other "worlds" the competitive games which here absorb the people's interest. These games, they claim, tighten the bonds between communities. That is to be proved. If two boxers have mutually demolished each other's jaw, I doubt that their spilled blood will create other than monetary ties.

In short, everything unites to place God in the heart of each home. And

112

being excommunicated in Rome literally amounts to being banned from society. It really amounts to no longer knowing what to believe or which way to turn. It's like leading the painful existence of the outcast. Being deracinated and cut off from bell tolls and the smell of incense... Faith is an unfathomable resource.

Certain men are so impolite that they stand on the doorsteps of their houses to observe me. The son calls the father, the father signals the mother, she the daughter, and soon it's a crowd elbowing or pinching each other.

A simple curiosity. One day Romans will understand that we don't live in a mythical country but in a country similar to theirs with sand, water, trees, animals and flowers. Undoubtedly they will discover, in amazement, that we are also horrified by lying, theft and murder. Especially they will understand that being a very old people like them, we now have a weakness for songs and dances, everything that gives back youth and the strength to continue the journey of existence. Preoccupied with living, helping each other, creating a warm community and with taking each others pulses, we haven't had the time to build temples of too cold and overly decorated marble to the Lord, temples peopled by majestic dead.

In their wanderings these Romans sought only the joy of living. And if it happened that they waged war with some of our neighbors, it's because they thought that with the spoils, they would bring back a little of their conception of existence. They departed with obelisks, which they erected on public places and lodged in certain of their churches. And yet it continues to be cold in their hearts.

"Felici faustoque ingressui!" Rome of juxtaposed cities, living neighborhoods and dead ones, men and ghosts, here everything intermingles, rubs shoulders and incites meditation.

* * *

Today, the anniversary of the death of Jesus Christ. Rome has gone into mourning. No balls, no movies. Nothing profane. Total recollection for a people. The only anniversary in which music and noisy crowds don't participate. An enormous sacrifice when one thinks that here joy and movement have a spontaneous and bubbling character because under this strange and at certain times bewitching sky, every noise is amplified and becomes music. Dance could easily turn into prayer. Just like at home.

And the fervor is such this evening that you would think that Rome, returning to her origins and seated at the feet of her god, wants to redeem Peter and establish unity between the slaves of yesterday and today.

Jesus comes back to Rome to be crucified anew.

113

Rome has adopted him and watched over him with jealous care. She wants the bread and the fishes to multiply and everyone to eat to his heart's content. In Jesus' temporal empire one cannot help but follow the Master's social principles.

* * *

Under a sky so beautiful as Rome's with women with such well-rounded angles, such engaging smiles, firey gazes and with such cordial handshakes, what sins couldn't be committed even if you called on all the Saints of Paradise for help! It suffices to be a little warm blooded and silly to glide very easily over one or the other of the commandments from Father God or Mother Church. The Roman who wouldn't want to offend anyone has moved for centuries in this labyrinth. That has given him such flexibility that he easily slips through your fingers. But the commandments are multiple, their meanings diverse and the hours caressing... So go and ask the imagination to restrain itself from leading you into tortuous paths. And Mother Church knows her children so well that every twenty-fifth year, the year of the Jubilee, all sins are solemnly remitted. A religious amnesty which brings the lost sheep back to the fold. Thinking themselves saved, the Roman people rest. Smiling they look at the newcomers on the international scene, and live within their ruins while polishing their titles of glory every morning. The gaze of men goes from destroyed temples to monuments still erect, from statufied emperors to those which fortune still misleads and applause exalts. They know you can conquer Rome, destroy it but without ever succeeding in erasing it from people's memory.

Let such a catastrophe happen unexpectedly, and a few days later, thousands of tourists would come running to see the place where Rome had been.

And then, why should a city over which angels and poets stand watch, die? Haven't the latter patiently filled the churches with works from their prodigious imaginations throughout the centuries? The Roman miracle is that next to the throne upon which money reigns, it was possible to make an honorable place for dreamers. The Roman people, who have a long history, found in taking inventory of it that what remains from their glorious past is not the great fortunes of the powerful men of that time, but really the works of the paladins that the poets are.

And the poets have penetrated these people so well that their actions have a peculiar character; in a city guide edited in the Parisian language, everything is mentioned except credit establishments. A modest veil thrown over monetary affairs, as if to say to the foreigner: "Let's talk about everything, except about what can divide us."

* * *

This evening I'm strolling down the streets in the company of a few friends. Light everywhere. Is this the most rational way of struggling against thieves? Is this a mania for seeing better at night than during the day or a struggle against the night of which they are undoubtedly afraid? To see how the people dance, we approach a policeman who tells us to go straight ahead, to turn left, to walk further, then turn right, the second street. Disquieting, this universal way of giving directions to the foreigner! If there had been a particular tree in front of the house, he would have mentioned it, exactly as we do. We thank him. He smiles and we do too. Who, in Rome, could refuse to smile? However the policeman's smile seems strange to me... Here we are in front of a violently lit sign: "American Night Club."[26] I understood the meaning of the policeman's malicious smile. Rome didn't dance on Good Friday night, but the Americans, they didn't ease up. Coming to Rome to see Americans dance took the cake. A sign lit up in a brutal, ostentatious way, discourteously and without regard for the surrounding lights, pointed up the power of American gold. This bar stares jauntily at you, snatches you up and pushes you into its belly to skin you. The American is growing up, his feet at home, his nose in the affairs of others and his hands in their pockets. A young, dynamic people, capable of clearing squared kilometers of land to build only upon a single acre.

American Night Club! You can't swear to anything in these civilized countries where everything intermingles and overlaps. Who is American? Who is Roman? Who will get this evening's returns? Our policeman must be laughing up his sleeve at having pushed us into American arms! Let pagan blacks go get fleeced by pagan Americans; himself a Roman, he washes his hands of it while thinking about the eventual benefits.

At the entrance, we deposit our raincoats in the cloakroom. Cost: a thousand liras. What a fabulous country America must be! We advance one behind the other following the old habit we have acquired from walking in narrow paths. And this fashion of walking in a single file has important consequences upon the stability of our societies. An old habit of walking in the footsteps of the elders, of not widening the roads for fear of frightening the gods posed along the path to count us and point out the foreigners for us. And how close you feel to one another on these narrow paths!

Waiters' heads bow to the right and to the left to greet us. I thought about the branches along the paths! In front of us, a large dance room, in back, a bar tended by a woman in an audaciously low-cut dress. She would have

115

gotten less attention nude. She seems unhealthily pale to me. It's as if she lacks sun, rain, wind and all those nothings which the skin needs in order to acquire its best tone. An unbecoming fruit very cleverly presented. Couples move around dancing the "cha cha!" a new dance which is revolutionizing these cold countries. An African rhythm carrying an American label. To land here, most of our articles pass through the hands of the Americans who sterilize them and give them a modern appearance. They purge them of all malaria and other tropical diseases, which frighten the white men terribly.

As we enter the door, three young ladies come to greet us and show us to a table. Cigarette in hand, body moulded in the dress, the beginning of breasts showing, like a trap.

A man rushes up to give us pieces of cardboard on which the price of the beverages are indicated. A well oiled mechanism, very American, a beautiful play in which each one conscientiously plays his role, with mastery.

To follow custom, we ask our companions who speak the Parisians' language to choose. Didn't I just miss my unique opportunity to show that among our people, the man chooses and the woman approves...discreetly. I am in an upside down world. All three of our companions choose champagne. That's good for us. You don't follow the traditions of others blindly. We look at each other. Champagne! Could I hesitate? Didn't I carry the reputation of our country's wealth on my frail shoulders? Is it up to me to tell these women that my country isn't as rich as they think it is? What would I have done to our honor? Isn't this bluffing time! Champagne! Oh well, let's go for champagne. "Alea jacta est!" I leaped head first into the expenses so as not to lose face. Let it not be said that one of our blacks had had an economic reaction. The leap, unfortunately, was going to be perilous, so deep and treacherous the gutter of a Roman American night club. The orchestra played softly out of respect for Good Friday. You would think that Jesus Christ still hanged from his cross on Golgotha.

My golden haired neighbor has a charming way of expressing herself. Her eyes reflect all the reflections from the bottles. She enjoys herself, searches for her expressions, and in order to urge them to come, she taps her head with her index finger. Just like we do when a name escapes us. Language of gestures! Inheritance which we drag through the centuries and which will allow us to find our way at a turn in the road!

I talk to her about our country, its gold, its diamonds, its precious wood, its lagoons, its good-tempered elephants and its always shining sun. She moves closer to me then as if I had suddenly become a star. Maybe she wants to smell the perfume of our forests and our fruits on me. She pulls herself together when I tell her of having left the country almost two months ago. I could no longer be arduous.

She found my indelible black coloring beautiful and wished she had the same color. The poor girl! She must not know anything about history! I'm not certain she reads newspapers: They aren't made to calm the readers. Here the charm of our existence bursts forth in all its splendor, ruled by seasons and never by the caprices of a press agent. The people on this continent lead a puppet existence that is cleverly regulated so they never wallow in quietude for too long. The journalists unceasingly brandish peace and war. Our companions drink and smoke without stopping. They call for more champagne. I look at them, dumbfounded. Look at them dance without making a single mistake. This assurance frightens me so much that I ask for the check: twenty-two thousand liras. Two half-bottles of champagne and a measly package of cigarettes. Obviously that seems expensive if one doesn't take into account the lighting, the low-cut dress, the orchestra, the smiles, the bows, the decoration and the owner's vacations. Here they have a strange way of calculating. They push the mania for recuperation to the point of asking clients to reimburse the price of a broom or a vacuum cleaner. Their reasoning is very absurd on this point. They claim that if they embellish their establishment, it's in order to honor the clientele. A very costly honor that has become a tradition which takes our breath away. "Red-hot" prices you have to accept like a well educated man. I believe that the world on this side of the ocean will one day need poorly educated men who can pour salt on certain wounds. If such customs ever crossed the ocean it's likely that they would turn the heads of thousands of our people and transform them into pleasure seekers, so malefic does the power of the lira seem to me.

The sign shines with victory. It is in complicity and in service. In order to shock you, the Roman from an old culture, pious and charitable, paying his tithes to the church and his taxes to the president, takes on the face of a barbarian, that of the American he intends to denigrate in the eyes of the travelers. This seller of Coca-Cola, rotten with money, undoubtedly doesn't have the Roman's friendship. How can anyone ask men who have suckled from the wolf to espouse a new regime without drawing their hate? The American who doesn't understand the Latin thinks that the abundance of American bars is a homage rendered to his culture. His very skillfully exploited vanity provides jobs for thousands of Romans who take after the Sibyl a little bit, and consequently deceive and confuse the brave American accustomed to seeing everything from the top of his six feet.

In the street, I calculated what precious things could have been bought with twenty-two thousand liras stoically invested in a double faced affair whose sign should have been "To the god Janus" and in subtitles "Americano-Roman bar."

The rain fell, fragile. Rome is crying for the entire world on this Good Friday. A car stops next to us and after several minutes of conversation carries away a woman. Two others remained leaning against a door, purses under their arms, braving the rain and cold. They puffed on their cigarettes. Are they Christians? Have they lost faith? To be born in the delicate smell of incense, in the middle of bell-tolls seeing thousands of pilgrims flocking to them and then to lose faith? By Saint Peter's beard! The papal blessings falling right and left upon Rome must have made all the plants grow, even the poisonous ones. And what price do they quote you for a screw with the night beauties? Seven thousand liras. You better believe that on Good Friday night, the prices in Rome reach the sky.

Seven thousand liras for a Roman woman! That's expensive. But when you think about her secular experience, about the glow in her eyes, about the calculated swing of her hips, about her lioness gait when walking, one can say that the Roman woman is sacrificed. Unmercifully sacrificed.

Men here, incapable of assuming their responsibilities, shirk them off on the woman who was supposed to have offered an old apple to an old ancestor. If she had eaten the apple all alone, the history of man would have taken another course. And to underline the woman's strength of character, they make her crush a snake's head with her feet. Terrible women.

In order to justify their fear, the Romans claim that their god condemns them to choose only one wife from among all the sirens that populate the country.

If by chance a Roman succeeded in living like us, not only would that pass for a monstrosity, but in his last moments, in spite of the children he would have had, the sacrifices made to raise them, the diplomacy displayed to make harmony reign between his naturally cantankerous co-wives, committing a final injustice, he would have to choose a veritable last companion. Evidently the god from here having taken only one rib from man doesn't tolerate him looking for it in the arms of several women. What implacable logic.

Luckily, the pagans and muslims don't go to the Roman paradise where everything happens as if in a barracks. Here, they have adopted a military god. They address soldiers' prayers to him.

* * *

Here we are in a small and very animated café. Men are talking, gesticulating, discussing, smoking, laughing, tapping each other on the shoulder and calling each other, exactly like at home. We order some Cinzano; the owner and the other clients are delighted. Each vies to talk the most and hold our attention the best.

Here we are far away from the American bar, among authentic Romans who are talking to us about their latest quarrel.

A young lady brings us coffee that they call "Expresso," a purely Roman recipe. We leave her the change. She hesitates; the blood rises to her face. I see her progressively change colors. Skin of glass, translucent. She whispers "grazie," but in a voice so sweet that this banal word seems to contain things that the "merci" of the Parisian waitress doesn't have. The Parisian "merci" is learned in books and correspondence courses. What gave this "grazie" such a musical accent is that everything here seems to be filled with real humanity. The men attempt to break away from the flow of time in order to chat joyously on her shores. They don't seem as if they are engaged in an exhausting competition with each other at all. Sometimes time slows down and strolls the length of a pleasant conversation, sometimes it flies very quickly by when the Roman doesn't want to work.

I had the impression that, having come in no hurry, the waitress had taken her time to say "grazie," had taken her time to clothe this word with a smile, and had taken her time to blush.

No sterile hurry in Rome where everything seems to conspire to wear out time itself, to harness it, to make it feverish with impatience and to urbanize it by putting a fishing pole in its hands and a pipe between its teeth. Why kill a time which comes to impale itself on the ramparts of its own accord.

Only a Roman woman, authentic, a descendant of vestal virgins could sing out with extasy:

I will wait day and night
I will always await your return.

The Roman language is full, sonorous and captivating. It can fill up the domes of cathedrals with its timbre, its waves, and its deep faith, and pursues its course into space in multicolored bubbles.

The fervor takes on such an opulent and pervasive form that if there were a village without bells, one could scream scandal. But, the mercantile spirit is such that you could find either a bone of Jesus or a thorn from his crown, or boiling blood or a crying virgin in such places to attract the crowds. A country where miracles are of abnormal frequency.

Faith in Rome is profitable considering the eagerness sellers of religious objects show in assaulting you.

Can anyone refuse a portrait of the Pope? Can anyone bargain about the price?

I think this tired people multiplies the decorations in order to conceal deficiencies.

What's admirable in their religious history is that the Son of their god, at no time, raised his hand against the apostle who betrayed him or the soldiers who brutalized him. But men seem to accord more importance to the insult suffered by the Master than to the lesson it taught. And since then, disciples of the Master of peace have armed themselves with swords which they brandish right and left, continuing to plant other martyrs along the road of charity. A way of bringing the sheep back to the fold.

Martyrs in the catacombs continue to produce. Tourists rush in columns to see them. Can anyone leave this country without seeing how the skeletons and hearts of these heroes interred during the night in underground cemeteries were made? So I joined a group of the curious. We go down a narrow staircase leading to a humid, poorly lit corridor similar to a footpath in the bush, where an indefinable odor reigns. All along the walls, to the right, to the left and from top to bottom, holes are hollowed out with bones still in most of them. But at the entrance an inscription damns whosoever should take any. Wise precaution. Ah! Why can't they leave heroes to rest who, for their faith, braved lions and tigers? In front of fifty-thousand spectators their blood spurted forth. Why can't they let them sleep in their humid galleries? Is it in order to perpetuate their sacrifice and associate it with that of Christ that Saint Peter's has such large proportions and dominates Rome? Is it in order to continue the resistance that Saint Peter's is surrounded by walls? Is it in order to hatch its chicks that it cuts itself off from the city? In order to remain a leaven? A goal? The barge on Rome's swelling waters? A reef of salvation? But where in the city aren't objects sold?...

Behind a window, a young girl looks at the street. She seems sad to me, waiting for a happiness that doesn't come. What is she dreaming about? Whom is she waiting for? The waiting pose is the same everywhere, some poke the fire and cry, others watch the door and the street, listen to the footsteps, voices and laughter. In their eyes, the same sadness, and on their shoulders, the same weight of solitude. The house seems too large, the lighting too garish and men selfish and happy. Time, too slow and the hours drag out. She has her nose glued to the window pane, contemplating what, no one knows. Can you be cold, feel alone in the holy city? I restrain myself from shouting to her: "You don't wait for happiness." We are trees which death strikes down and misfortunes defoliate. In every moment, let's gather the small parcel of laughter and forgetfulness that it contains. No god has cursed the earth or rationed out happiness. I wanted to shout to her that at home health is the most eminent of fortunes.

So don't glue your nose to the window unless to admire the human fresco and to listen to the city's murmuring. The earth is an immense workshop which is going to buzz with happy tunes...

A crippled old man approaches me:

— You American?

— No, I'm African...Parisian!

— Ah!... Paris is beautiful, I love Paris, I adore Paris, I dream only of Paris.

— A marvelous city. I was there a week ago.

He almost threw his arms around my neck.

— You have just come from there! Give me your hand.

The most beautiful city in the world. Rome is nothing next to Paris, and I'm Roman. Before the war, that damned war which "took" one of my legs, I was an actor. So I played in Paris, London, Berlin and in many other cities. But Paris is unique, it's a jewel; I would like so much to go back. I don't like Rome... Isn't it the desire to meet people that incites us to leave our villages and our countries?

I looked at the woman behind the window. My interlocutor followed my eyes, smiled and continued:

— She's beautiful but there are some even more beautiful. I could show them to you. We are in a paradise of beautiful women here.

We entered a café where we drank a Cinzano, talking all the time about Paris. I watched two waitresses whose hair seemed to cast soft reflections upon the clients maneuvering between the tables and behind the counter. Small colored headbands held back their hair, the dresses were moulded to their figures, accenting everything that could make men's heads turn. My gaze went from the bottles in all shapes, the liquers in all colors, candies, cakes and sausages to the bodies of the waitresses who seemed to work without touching the ground. I looked around me with all my pores open. Did my neighbor think I was overwhelmed with solitude, nostalgia? Leaning towards me, he whispered:

— Do you want some...

— No, I say, shaking my head.

This clear and prompt answer disarmed him. It was undoubtedly the first time he had met a tourist who didn't want some...which he should taste like a regional specialty. I think I hurt his feelings. You just don't respond so flatly to a proposition, especially when in Rome, where eloquence flourishes, and there are thousands of ways to disguise the truth, dress the lie to present a refusal. The Machiavelism of men is endless. On the one hand they liberate the women and on the other they enclose her in houses which they themselves call special. The most astonishing thing is that the woman accepts being exploited. Is it the maternal fibre which makes her accept the role? You never know from which side to approach the people here, they're so changeable. By dint of synthesizing everything and suggesting everything, they have succeeded in losing sight of realities and so they no longer seem always to have their feet on the ground. I wouldn't swear that they haven't also lost sight of man, that they don't liken him to a simple mechanism in the gigantic set of gears which is their society. A simple bolt which can be replaced. A society which is more frightening than our thickest forests. It's in these countries that I have understood to what extent wealth can divide men, put them at odds with each other, make them aggressive and inhuman. Undoubtedly it isn't by accident that Jesus was born here in the direst poverty.

We leave the inn. The young girl still had her nose glued to the window. A Roman woman who no longer understood Rome and its language of images. What could other countries bring her that Rome doesn't have? Another illusion of freedom, of apparently broader perspectives? But they would be so limited. Can another sky be more deep, more sonorous than Rome's sky whose air nonetheless secretes a caress at certain hours that is as warm as that of the Holy Spirit Bank notes? She's forgetting that in no other part of the world is there an Appian Way bordered by restaurants where in the evenings one can dine in the company of Scipion, Horace, Curiatti, Seneca, Cecilia, Metilla and under the flame of the cypress trees.

She doesn't know that she possesses the most beautiful fountain in the world, the Trevi toward which the tourists rush.

In order to win the good graces of the fountain's spirits, they throw them small change. No one knows anymore how this practice, which is apparently very old, was born.

What a look into time, beyond the men who direct the present seated in secular armchairs! What is this young girl with her nose glued to the window thinking? Another enigma in Rome, among the ruins of fountains, palaces and temples!

With extreme prudence, the Ruins of Rome speak as do the elders at home, in a Sibylian language. To the powerful, intoxicated by the incense of praises and filled more each day with their infallibility, they whisper: "Chi va piano, va sano,"[27] and to the small people, groaning under the weight of their burdens and for whom night and day are nothing but darkness, they say: "Quos vult perdere Jupiter dementat"[28] while pointing out with fingers nibbled off by time the most important among them.

The men here are so superstitious that they don't like to bring a foreigner into their home. So they meet him in restaurants or public places where the bad spirits can't operate.[29] Unfounded supposition since it happens that the proprietors of these establishments go bankrupt. Following a custom which is just as strong as in our country, an Admiral friend and his two nieces whisk me down streets, sometimes wide and sometimes narrow, towards a restaurant of their choice. A restaurant whose character is the sum of the character of all the other restaurants. How many things I saw that I no longer remember! Was this due to the exceptionally pleasant, caressing weather, to the presence of two smiling female friends? They pointed out the main thoroughfares and monuments and then all of a sudden they laughed together. And I did the same. The streets, monuments and signs! What do these silent things become when you are close to a Roman woman who is talking to you, listening to you, and then bursts out laughing with all her teeth showing? In such company, I could have traveled round the world without feeling the least bit tired.

The taxi lets us out in front of a restaurant that is discreetly luxurious.

The Roman people no longer seem to like gaudiness or indecent luxury. Marble and gildings no longer dazzle them. On the contrary, they seem to disturb them. We enter a crowded and smoke-filled room. Many of the diners had finished eating and were digesting their meal with cigarettes or pipes in their mouths. Imagination is evident again in the table arrangements: no cords or angles. The heart?

Rome no longer bothers with mathematical rigor.

The Admiral's popularity is such that upon entering, heads straighten up, and everyone greets him, smiling. We take a table in the back of the room. A mischievous waiter hands me the menu. I ask him to read it to me. As he doesn't understand me, we all burst out laughing. Face was saved. Everyone had shown his ignorance. The Admiral wanted to offer me a dish, C... a dish of peas and F ... a shellfish dish, each dish being a specialty from a specific region. All three are so nice. Whom should I displease? My stomach has its limit. We get around the difficulty with a very Roman diplomacy. I'll eat a portion of each of their dishes.

Charming company! You would think we had known each other for years. At dessert time, an accordionist and a guitarist come with their songs to enliven the room. Clowns attached to no one, neither a king, a prince, nor a powerful courtesan. They follow the whims of their imagination, like non-salaried poets. And everyone welcomes them with a smile. Especially the lovers who want to have a lasting memory of an evening out. They excel in the art of reciting and telling stories. Romans think very highly of them and pay them accordingly. They sang about those who were in the room and one word was repeated over and over again: "le farfalle...le."[30] The room, drunk with joy, clapped hands to accompany them. What! They clap hands in this country too, just as we do when accompanying a singer!

And I thought that they had passed this elementary stage in the expression of joy! Could the Romans be blacks who have strayed over here?

—Le farfalle...le..."

The song must be popular. The melody is nostalgic. And I'm seeing again the woman who had her nose glued to the window. Observing the women's gazes, the slow breathing which lifts up their bosom, and the attention that they pay to the singers, one is convinced that the words are filled with tenderness. The girl next to me translates them for me.

— It's "The Song of the Butterfly," she tells me.

Delicate butterfly
Colored butterfly
White and yellow butterfly
It's the flower of the sky
And the star of God the Father

Silent butterfly
Mysterious butterfly
It's the lucky-charm
Of all lovers
Under the full moon

Finally, I have the key. I'm going to be able to understand Rome! How long I've been turning around the citadel, like a neophyte! Nowhere did the guards open the doors: Porta Angelica, Porta Pia, Porta del Popolo, Porta Latina. The same deafness everywhere. I was missing the password "Butterflies!" All of a sudden I grasped the Roman personality, the woman's attitude at the window, the waitresses' glide between tables, and the dance step of the waiter in the restaurant. That a whole people takes its time and submits the hours to its caprices, doesn't astonish me anymore.

This butterfly on a billboard at the entrance of the city and the popular song called Song of the Butterfly. This is Rome! A butterfly which has perched itself upon time.

* * *

— Have you seen the Pope? asked the Admiral after the song ended.
— No, I say.
— You must see him, it's essential.

At that point I had the painful impression that this venerable old man was placed among the vestiges from ancient times. To come to Rome without seeing the Pope! In Paris I had already heard someone say to another person: "And what's more, if you aren't satisfied, go see the Pope!" I'm not satisfied either. So am I going to miss the chance to tell him everything I have on my chest?

* * *

I left "Caesar Augustus" for a boarding house right in the center of the city. The emperor, having been transformed into a sign and a guard, watched me indifferently as I took my taxi. He had seen enough of my head. It undoubtedly looked like those of the men who, at the time of his triumphs, shouted to him, ceaselessly: "Look behind you." "Remember what you were." Beautiful Roman wisdom which tries to restrain man on the borderline of conceit.

In this quarter, houses, ochre in color, have stories. It's an old, respectable quarter; no washing hangs at the window; no noise in the evenings; the shutters are careful not to shine. A silent doorway, a carpet, and a monumental marble staircase. It's in this house that I was to lose face, among old people who took pains not to bump into any piece of furniture. I was listening to the city's muted noise from my window when Mireille, bringing her hand to her mouth to explain the meaning of her sentence, came to shout to me from the door: "mantjore."[31] I thought about the succulent dishes consumed in the company of the Admiral and his two nieces. When you have such pleasant memories "in the stomach" you readily run toward the table that is shown to you. That's what I did. The old woman to the right and two other old women in the company of an old man to the left. In front of me, at the back table, another old woman. It's frightening how many old people there can be in Roman houses! Aren't they ghosts, especially since they hardly make any noise and barely speak to each other!

Between the mouthfuls we tried to smile at each other. Each person, conscientiously, with a sustained effort, drank his soup, making very sure that the spoon did not touch the bottom of the plate. A majestic silence, which is part of the menu, helps digestion, adds to the quarter's majesty and to the boarding house's serious atmosphere. Then the spaghetti came. Sweat wet my back and forehead. To what corner of Rome can you go without meeting up with spaghetti. I'm alone, in open country, totally unprotected. You have to engage a battle with an adversary who imposes his strategy upon you. I dared not put down my weapons even though that would have been wise. And Mireille, as if to tease me, had put the dish under my nose, a dish of spaghetti with tomato sauce. She looked at me, little Mireille, with black eyes. She served me in spite of myself, allowing me the possibility however to raise my arms and say: enough.

We looked at each other in silence. I rolled up my sleeves, the spaghetti remained unabashed. Had I come so far to lose a battle? I had to cross this other Rubicon and show Rome that at home we all have courage enough to spare. I seized my knife and cut up these long worms, yellowed with tomato sauce, into small pieces. Then I gathered them up with my spoon, pushing them with the flat edge of the knife. The neighbors, shocked, watched me out of the corner of their eyes. I defied them ostensibly by raising my knife and cutting off the last spaghetti soldier's head. The fork of one of the old ladies froze in mid-air, an old man opened his mouth in astonishment, Mireille elbowed the second waitress and the two of them started laughing while pretending to be telling funny stories to each other. I held my knife in hand, determined to conquer Rome, all Romans and all spaghetti. At one point, old men and women put down their forks and biscuits, wiped their mouths and smiled. I understood that I had tried their patience, that they had had enough of seeing me act in such a barbarian way with the national dish. Their pride revolted. Everyone watched me load my spoon with arms, thighs, heads and ears of spaghetti. Between two mouthfuls, I tried to gaze at Mireille to decipher what she was saying to her neighbor. Eyes stayed fixed on me. The Romans must admit that spaghetti can be eaten in several ways and not just rolled around a fork.

These eyes, these smiles! I lost confidence in myself...my hand hesitated, my neck no longer stretched out as fast...my lips stayed closed. My tablecloth was all red with blood.

Mireille looked at me smiling. Here one always smiles even when one disapproves of a gesture. The old Romans forgot to eat, the massacre filled them with waves of the holy angel that leads to Crusades. Then noses bent down upon the plates. I was weighed, judged and condemned. The people no longer paid any attention to me. Dagger high, I kept struggling, smiling, happy to be cutting up their spaghetti. I want to adapt this national dish to my ways. It's important that it can be eaten in another way besides the Roman way.

Maliciously, the maids left the same tablecloth on the table to show everyone that I ate the spaghetti in a revolting way. Too bad!

Each person, when going back to his room, whispered "buona sera."[32] I put up a front in vain, I was ashamed of my tablecloth. Executioner of the national dish, I tried to be the last one to leave; the group of two old women and an old man, vigilant guardians of tradition, wouldn't let me. After the dessert, after tea, after the medicines, they stayed there, talking and telling each other a thousand stories. Before getting up, I folded over a corner of the tablecloth to make the maids understand that they could change it for me. This sign, clear to us, was incomprehensible to them. Every morning I found the same tablecloth again, even more red than the night before. I looked Mireille in the eyes. She lowered them. I tried to talk to her. She answered in monosyllables. All this to make me understand that it was time to leave Rome. The dirty tablecloth, the smiles which had become more bitter and more condescending, got on my nerves. The "buona sera" and the "bon giorno" addressed to me increased because everyone had classified me: the barbarian in the city.

However, I was able to visit one of the places where the Romans accumulate war collections: weapons, materials, drums, utensils, cowry shells, pottery, etc. Paintings representing atrocious scenes of villages, hilltops and waterways being taken. Cannons lined up and labeled, shine with cleanliness. In the "war" section at the end of a long corridor where tanks and photographs of soldiers are displayed, a placard reads:

Adua 1st March 1896
Adua 5th May 1936

Forty years after, the Very Holy Rome which adorns itself with sacred texts had washed an old defeat in blood. The soldiers, upon leaving, must have received a special blessing; soldiers of Law, Charity and Justice, they were to bring the lost sheep back to the fold, those who talk to God in a language other than the Roman dialect. The Romans like most of the peoples on this continent don't know the shortcuts to which we are accustomed and they blow everything up to their proportions. One day we will have to help them get themselves together, to be content and to make room for others. Certainly this will be difficult, after all of their conquests, all the more so since Cato the Elder lives again in each citizen.

I had proof of such tenacity through one of the numerous vendors who people Republic Square. I was walking when I was joined by a man who had been following me for a while. Approaching me, he took a package from the pocket of his jacket.

— Sir...

— What...

— Cameos, he says while showing me a chain, a bracelet, two earrings, a ring...

A beautiful set of women's jewelry in pink cameo. Tempted, I said no anyway, for fear of being cheated.

—Four thousand liras.

I made a face. That gave him courage. A psychologist, he knew that a man who makes a face under such circumstances is a potential client.

— Look how beautiful it is. In the stores it would cost 15 thousand liras. As for us, we make them ourselves. So we can sell them at very little profit, and sometimes we even given them away for nothing.

— Too expensive...

— Do you think so? A once in a lifetime opportunity. In Paris you would pay through the nose for them. I know Paris, myself...

— No, I don't want them, I say with the tone of an undecided man, struggling against himself.

— Here, look, give them a good going over. Imagine them on the neck, arms, ears and finger of your wife, and think about your wife adorned with all of that in a mirror... A simple effort of the imagination I know you are capable of... It's not expensive, Sir! Anything that enhances a woman's beauty is never too expensive... Beauty, you know, doesn't have a price... A once in a lifetime opportunity. You'll regret it; think it over, really think about it while envisioning your wife, seeing her adorned with this marvelous necklace, this divine ring... Cameos are the jewelry of goddesses, sir! Three thousand liras!... Your wife will be grateful to you for the rest of her life...

— I don't want any.

I was lying; if the vendor had left, I would have looked for him, but everyone had to play his game honestly without falling in the other person's trap.

I hastened my step so as not to be conquered. When an adversary loses confidence in himself, the conqueror notices it; and my vendor followed at my heels, determined to finish me off. No mercy! He had been following me for 45 minutes, in front of restaurants, parks, fountains and in gardens. Somewhat of a nuisance of a neighbor.

— Ah! I understand you... Never!... We make them ourselves. Have no fear, since we feel free to sell them in public under the nose of the police. Here, look at them in the light, in the bright light... and make up your mind!...

He put the package in my hands, then refused to take it back. The last ramparts crumbled within me. Accustomed to taking positions, he[33] watched me smiling, savoring his victory. I hesitated.

— Three thousand liras. It's a gift I'm offering you.

— Two thousand liras.

— O.K.... take it

I had won! A two thousand lira discount. Progress... I had just beat a Roman on his ground and in his own city, under the eyes of his Lares gods. I was beginning to frighten myself. What would I become at this pace, at the end of a month? What merchant could sell me something? Finally, I had my revenge upon the spaghetti.

Just when the man pocketed the money, a quick glint of joy, very quick, but how significant, lit up his face. This glint immediately made me worried... I had undoubtedly just been cheated again. Ah, these Romans, completely round and offering hardly any angles to grasp them by. I understood that I could have continued to bargain, to bargain without stopping, until one of us had no saliva left or took off at break-neck speed so as not to be conquered. I was furious because of it. Bargaining for nearly an hour and falling into the trap! Ah, these decendants from the wolf, always elusive! On what ground will I be able to win a victory, oh! the smallest victory, any victory; a ground here in Rome which would be neutral and give me a chance? I saw my dirty table cloth again and felt crushed by Rome, its ruins, its lights, its movement, its merchants, its buildings, by everything and everyone united against me.

"Felici faustoque ingressui!" Only the drivers had mercy upon me. Now I also understood the meaning of the old people's smile when I joyously massacred the spaghetti: they left up to others to correct me. Who could pretend to always understand the meaning of an old person's smile? I took it as an adoption, and here a small merchant teaches me a profound lesson, makes me realize just how far the Roman unity extends.

I was pondering my revenge when I was approached by a second vendor who presented me with cameos in a different color. Thank God, I had the unique opportunity to show my real wares. We're going to be able to join arms. A brilliant revenge within my reach, a thunderous revenge which will leave all the Romans and their gods, and all the very shrewd and marvelously organized merchants amazed. Now I knew their weak spot.

— Three thousand liras...

— I already have some.

— It's not the same thing... Show me what you have...

— It's the same color.

— No, I bet that it's different...

— How do you know?

— I just do! my merchant's shrewdness.

— In any case, I don't want any of your cameos.

— A piece of advice, all cameos aren't the same, the way they're cut gives them an undefinable something that distinguishes them. Let me see what you have.

— No, leave me alone.

This sharp tone hardly discouraged my merchant.

— Three thousand liras for these marvelous, good-luck cameos.

I entered a store, the vendor followed me there. I left to go into Saint Mary of the Angels Church. I was going to beg her to come to my assistance, to help me win a small victory in Rome where I had begun to doubt myself. A half hour looking, regaining strength. I bought two rosaries so as to put myself in the holy graces of the Madonna of the Angels. I thought that I had gotten rid of, discouraged my beseiger. That was really underestimated. A small Roman vendor, an authentic descendant of Cato the Elder. He waited for me at the exit, very relaxed, smiling and more enterprising than ever. What must one do to discourage a Roman? I tensed my muscles so as not to fall into his trap but on the other hand determined to catch him in mine.

— Have you really thought about it? Three thousand liras, beautiful cameos. Once in a lifetime chance! Look, they have a finish which you'll never find anywhere else in the whole country. We make them according to an old, secret method passed down from father to son. Compare them with yours...

I still refused and for two hours strolled around the city. Upon returning to Republic Square, who approaches me? the same vendor, a disarming calm, the same smile manufactured in who knows what factory. He was beating me by wearing me down.

— Three thousand liras. A gift, sir.

So I decided to play the big game, to accept the challenge, to prove to him that we also know how to fight. He sensed my determination and smiled more, the malicious smile of a man savoring his victory in advance. So, calling on all the gods for help, I affronted my merchant...

— How much?

—Three thousand liras.

—No, one thousand liras.

— Two thousand. For you, I'll agree to a thousand lira sacrifice.

— A thousand!... You see, I tell him while taking out the first package, I don't need any more cameos.

Decisive argument, but one which doesn't stop a Roman seller. Mine responded calmly:

— It's not the same color. You gave two thousand liras to the other vendor. Take mine for one thousand five hundred liras. That will make your wives very happy.

— I have only one wife, according to Roman law.

— Ah, you're Christian?

— Yes...

— That's very good. So you understand that cameos are very expensive and...

— But what would I do with two cameos?

— You undoubtedly have a sister...

— I don't have any.

— Surely a girlfriend...

— None...

— Anyway, a little souvenir from Rome, that always makes anyone happy, not counting the fact that it brings good luck... Everything here is blessed...

— If you'd make a gift of it to me, I'll pray for you to all of the gods from my country...

— The gods from your country, my merchant responded smiling, but they no longer understand your language since you're Roman Catholic...

— No, we get along very well and we understand each other perfectly. We've cohabited together for centuries...

—You could also offer cameos to them...

—A thousand liras.

The merchant burst out laughing and with his index finger pushed back the visor of his cap. I'm winning my victory!... But this face!... This face...

— One thousand five hundred liras.

— No, one thousand liras, I say categorically.

— Give it here!...

Ah! I have it, my victory. Finally, a point chalked up. A victory. The man opened the package, counted and recounted the ring, the necklace, the earrings and the bracelets in front of me, closed the package again, and handed it to me. I put it in my pocket and very joyously, handed him in turn, a thousand lira bill. We shook hands as loyal fighters.

Finally, a Roman beaten, defeated, a Roman who bent his knees!

In order to taste my victory, feast upon it, I sat down in front of a café. Finally I felt equal to all the Romans who strolled around in front of me. I felt the need to rub elbows with all the passersby so as to measure my strength. Very happy to have pulled off this masterful coup, I slowly took out my package from my pocket, opened it ceremoniously, counted and recounted. I was missing the ring and an earring. And yet, he had put them in the package. I dug in my pockets, turned them inside out... the ring and the earring were missing.

After such a feat, on what other ground could I expect to struggle against a Roman? Two overwhelming defeats in the same day, after the daily victory which the spaghetti had inflicted upon me! Henceforth, I was afraid of the children who, on the Janiculus, tell you they haven't eaten since morning. An easy way of selling their post cards to you.

What can you do against men who wear down time itself?

* * *

Gregorius XII, Pont. Max.

Sixtus V, Pont. Max.

Clemens XII, Pont. Max.

The Rome of Popes! Why does everyone ask me if I've seen the Pope? I understand the meaning of the struggle that two forms of civilization are fighting here. The first, static, dreaming of privileges; made for clients or stockholders in the Bank of the Holy Spirit or the Bank of Rome. The second, dynamic, wants to teach man to think less about his stomach and his skin. It upsets the old vision that makes up the strength of a world, of a continent. It undermines what one could call "europocentrism."

Is it by accident that banks and prisons were born under this country's sky? That candies and whips are put in the hands of God and that the Pope has the keys to heaven and hell?

Hasn't a trembling, chilly, shaky faith been given to all the pilgrims who sell rosary beads, kiss medals, climb stairs on their knees, kneel before sarcophagi, and rush into catacombs? Don't they live in constant fear instead of having a healthy faith in their God? Doesn't the humble manger throw discredit upon the gilded buildings? Don't the grandiose temples incite Christians to run after wealth? What a leaf-gilded civilization, yet one which has lived by plunder and pillage!

* * *

So I succeeded in seeing the Pope. His palace is one of the city's largest monuments. The pilgrims' footsteps have polished the never-ending marble of the staircases. Suspicious and inquisitorial porters in front of a bronze door carefully sort out those who want to see the Very Holy Father. Could he also have enemies? The line here is meditative, but very pushy and packed together. I bet the same scene undoubtedly happens daily at the entrance to paradise. A motley crowd of people risen from all the tombs, all the columbariums, all the cemeteries—some in rags, some in full dress—in a hurry to leave earth.

Saint Peter observes the heads, weighs the hearts, takes the temperature of convictions and digs into the minds so that no subversive idea gets past. The heavenly frontier! If one must be in paradise to work like a horse, one can maintain that the very honorable Saint Peter has only changed lands. A plain, excuse me, a large cemented court yard, a fountain and a clock imbedded in the wall. Soldiers angelically stand guard. Their rifles must be made of wood. Smiling soldiers, it's just for fun. What war can they win in such shining attire in an era of camouflage?

Because, here, men no longer know which animals to imitate. They have panther colored clothes and tiger colored ones. They no longer want to remain men but want to return to the animals of the bush. It's hard to fathom what instinct calls them, but the attraction is so strong that there are many who like to play at being animals, in the middle of the city. The people admire them and consider them heroes. Evidently, becoming an animal is a real feat. There are many who like to play at being predators. There are corporations of leopard men, panther men and tiger men. And no one realizes the regressions that they are undergoing by this mutation. Man's condition weighs them down so much that they are returning to their origins. The Pope's soldiers are so conscious that they have wooden guns, that they don't stop smiling.

More stairs. A peaceful ascent towards the sky... like a joyous troop. Teasers continue to take away the solemn character of the march. Maniacs full of life, who even before Saint Peter can't restrain themelves from provoking general laughter with a sentence or a gesture.

We emerge upon a large room, all in marble and filled with frescoes. A warm room. Angels, saints, colors... It really makes you want to win paradise in order to lounge around in such a sumptuous decor. The guide turns left. A narrow door. A cloakroom where you leave everything that could be inconvenient in an interview with a great man. We are now in a smaller room: the Consistory, the place of the Very Holy Father's apparatus. Gilded ceiling and facing the Pope's gilded throne, a Christ with a gilded angel at his feet. It's no longer surprising that men here placed so much importance upon gold; their whole paradise is gilded and they intend to build themselves gilded houses so as to make earth a second paradise. Doesn't doing away with gold amount to taking away their whole reason for living? Gold fascinates them; now if a man doesn't shine, how can he have a place in their hearts? Women steadfastly refuse to give birth to golden men!

Behind the throne, a crimson red tapestry. On the dark violet walls are painted, besides the weapons, seven allegorical panels and an eagle with spread wings. Lion, panther, eagle, it's toward these summits that men gravitate. Did the birds of prey change character upon entering this majestic room?

Two loudspeakers, a microphone, movie directors and official photographers. Machines alone can capture the Pope in the proper light. Harmony between modernism and archaism. All the jolts and revolutions die at the walls of the citadel, from above which the Very Holy Father stands watch. Long-robed cardinals come and go. At every moment you think you see the Very Holy Father appear more red than the others and more laden with gold. I was observing the golden angel at the feet of the nearly nude Christ on his cross when there was a movement in the room and applause broke out. I stood up. Dressed in white, a venerable old man who struggled vigorously against time, determined to lead his flock as far as possible, had just appeared, blessing the crowd that we were. The Pope! Time respected him: no wrinkle on his face. He was an old, smiling grandfather who welcomed his grandsons. This was not the one who makes you wait for years while a problem is resolved; the one who, attentive to praises, is easy to anger when a truth is uttered to him. He is, moreover, infallible. The contrary would have been surprising since he is God's living representative on earth. Men needed this rallying point because they have so burdened their God with beard, centuries and rheumatisms. Ours is ageless and wants no humiliation for us.

Not a fly buzzes. This sacred place isn't made for such bugs. There are heights which they can't attain.

The Pope speaks in a sure, pleasant voice without emphasis. He has, they say, such understanding towards his collaborators that doctors examine them to uncover any diseases they might be carrying. This concern for man on this continent of machines and gears makes the Very Holy Father grow in our eyes. He even wins over those who refuse to be in his flock.

The Pope stands up. A spring pushes us towards him, hands extended. The cardinals, frightened by such an explosion of fervor, convinced that a very old instinct could be awakened, encircle the Very Holy Father. The Pope calmly admires the teeth that we show him. We clap hands and he blesses us. Dignified, he returns to his apartments. In the cloak room, we take back our coats, our hats and all our customs. Here in the Vatican time hasn't passed since the memorable encounter between Jesus and Peter on the Appian Way. This way of considering time in its unity, in its global duration, bestows a great serenity upon everyone. Those who work in this citadel think themselves immortal.

I have seen the Pope. The past, present and eternity converge.

* * *

"Qui non si muore mai."[34] How can you die when you are perched upon time? When one knows how to conform to the roll of the waves and the rigidity of the peaks?

I have seen the Vatican, the forum, the Capitol, the Coliseum, Saint John's of Lateran, Michelangelo's Moses showing his wound on the right knee, Cecilia Metella's tomb, the Borghese Villa. What sums up all of man's tumultuous history is the bronze angel on the summit of the Holy Angel castle. Prophets raise the sword. Eagles spread their wings, even on the walls of the Consistory. The old angel of extermination puts the sword back in the sheath.

This is the greatest lesson that one can and must take from Rome.

The eternal city has just given me new proofs of its perenniality. A people who want to be free of all restraints even if they happen to be ruthless in money matters. A people who see gold as a means, can submit to all restrictions, head held high, hands clean, with light hearts and a song on their lips. What else can you do under this sky but sing and call others to form the circle?

This morning, when leaving the boarding house, I had to remind the proprietor that I owed him money for two laundered shirts and three telephone calls. Not only did he not make me pay these, but he called a taxi for me at his own expense.

In the shipping companies' waiting room, a sales woman consented to my "getting rid of" my money, by making me a two hundred lira reduction on an article I bought. In Paris, under the same circumstances, I was urged with bright smile to go to the marketplace where prices could be discussed. Parisian rigor is generously moderated in Rome. Bagatelle, I agree. Just an argument about numbers. Yet that characterizes a man, a people, a nation. A generous people isn't one who calculates the extent of its generosity but one who accomplishes it because the heart commands it. Here, people don't always seem to dwell needlessly on the significance of a gesture, the essential thing being that it brings comfort and joy.

Rome liberates man and with one finger points out the past, the present and the deep sky to him. It's up to him to understand and to situate himself.

I've even seen a guide negligently throw down beside him the money tourists give him. He seemed to be embarrassed to touch it. His mission was to show Rome, the Catacombs, the Protestant cemetery. It's up to us to seize the long and painful history of human relationships. He was an apostle and not an employee, a bard, a priest at his altar, microphone in hand. Even at night, he would be ready to show you his country. For him time is a sometimes heavy companion who crushes palaces and marble temples, pulverizes statues of false gods and reestablishes equilibrium.

* * *

As he was about to take the plane, a tourist dug in his pockets to get rid of his last Roman coin. Rome freed him from all servitude. He was ecstatic. He seemed happy to be leaving this country of ruins, of talkative and ceremonious policemen. He was a weakling who hadn't been able to stand Rome's heady wine and who was taking extreme measures to pull himself together. On his tongue he had the fizzle of "Lambrusco"[35] and at the corners of his lips, the little smile of "grignolino."[36] He was fleeing Rome which had conquered him in spite of himself.

As for myself, I couldn't help thinking about "The Song of the Butterfly," about the angel who put the sword back into the sheath thus putting intelligence and power at everyone's disposal, about the saleswoman's gesture, about the Pope, so ancient and so present.

Vividly I saw again, on the antique Appian Way where the fountain no one dares turn off still runs, the inn which had as its sign: "Here, no one dies." The wind whistled through the cypress trees as in the era of the emperors, as at the moment when Peter met Christ.

"Qui non si muore mai!"

Here no one dies.

What certitude and superb confidence in the sign of the inn on the Appian Way!

Sibyl can be quiet, and desert her cavern, there will always be good fairies to lean over cribs and make the child smile.

And the child who smiles is weather that clears, the future that is illuminated, life that bursts into bloom; it's the angel who shoves his sword deeper into the sheath, so that skies in Rome and other places will be filled with laughter and songs.

On the old, imperial way the sign becomes brighter:

"Qui non si muore mai!"

Rome March 24 - April 3, 1959

NOTES

[1] The narrator immediately establishes one of the bases upon which his distance from Parisian society is founded. It results from an irreconciliation of Western abstraction, technical pragmatism and artificiality with a certain African spirituality, humaneness and naturalness. This theme of abstraction versus spirituality is treated in many works of African fiction, notably in Cheikh Hamidou Kane's *Aventure Ambigüe*.

[2] This phrase exemplifies the relationship of the implied narrator's point of view to that of the author. By using the expression, for example, "in that country" instead of "in my country," Dadié makes a technical distinction between his personal observations as author and his observations as narrator. Such a narrative position gives the impression of a more objective point of view. Dadié's use of this narrative distancing is seen structurally in his *Climbié* where the position of the narrator changes from the first person in Part I to the third person in Part II. This establishment of a narrative distance between the author's point of view and that of the implied narrator is an important aspect of Dadié's style.

[3] Here irony is directed toward the French language as a social phenomenon. Today, French is upheld by many and often lauded as a beautiful, tightly structured and complex language. It is not uncommon, however, for African languages which are just as complex to be referred to, by many, as dialects. Thus the irony results from the narrator's term of comparison. He uses a reversal technique by adopting a traditional Western attitude toward African languages and applying it to the French language.

[4] The English translation does not capture the exactness of the narrator's relationship to his audience; this is shown stylistically in the French text. The original reads: "Ce terme de troupeaux pourrait, à juste raison, t'offusquer..." By using the "tu" form, the narrator at once expresses his familiarity with his audience and his close relationship to it. The English "you" fails to show this rapport. The same close relationship is manifested in the African oral tradition between the story-teller and the

audience. Through his style Dadié thus introduces this aspect of oral tradition into a modern form.

[5]Cowry shells were once used as money in parts of Africa.

[6]The French text reads: "Les mots nous forment et conditionnent nos actes (p.21)." The idea is that words, through such conditioning, can keep us from seeing reality for what it is. To be clearly understood, Dadié's point of view must be seen within the framework of the African concept of the word (Nommo) according to which "the enunciation produces what it names. Naming is an incantation, a creative act. What we cannot conceive of is unreal; it does not exist. But every human thought, once expressed becomes reality."* Dadié, however, takes a more critical view of language and the whole concept of Nommo. He shows an extreme sensitivity to the tendency of language to distort, rather than create reality.

*Janheinz Jahn, Muntu, The New African Culture, trans. Majorie Greene (New York: Grove Press, 1961), p. 133.

[7]Emphasis is placed upon serious observation throughout the narrative. Visual images are developed in such a way as to include every possibility included in the situation. Such elasticity allows the observer to manipulate space while remaining attached to a particular point in time and to a specific image. In this example, Dadié extends the image of the black walking with a loaf of bread under his arm to include a commentary upon a certain social and historical situation. Later on in the text a drop of rain fallen upon the observer's nose is extended into a mythical struggle between the nose and the rain (see p. 64).

[8]In developing the image of the rabbi, the narrator includes a definition of literary terms important to Dadié's non-fiction: "Oh, but what are books, if not accounts of experiences or attempted dreams?" Each of his chroniques, Un Nègre à Paris, Patron de New York and La Ville où nul ne meurt (Rome) centers around the experiences and dreams of one central character.

[9] Concession is better left untranslated for it shows Dadié's manipulation of language. In French concession means a grant or plot of land; in this context the same word means home or community.

[10]"Accourue, je ne sais pas d'où, une vieille histoire racontée par un ami parisien bondit en moi." The use of the verb accourir (to come running up to) and the verbal phrase bondir en moi (to jump up inside me) are important to create the effect of a narrative in constant movement and a universe in which even inanimate objects and abstractions have an autonomous existence and morality of their own. The English translation does not convey this movement.

[11]"Bac" is a shortened form of baccalauréat, the diploma received after one has passed the rigorous examinations terminating study in the lycée or secondary school.

[12]The narrator's reference to temporal continuity expresses a oneness with the total universe not seen in contemporary Western societies. Concommitant with his living in a world of abstraction and technology, Western man is bound by arbitrary and restrictive time structures. Such divisions deny complete cosmic unity.

[13]There seems to be an obvious misprint in the text where "différend" instead of "différent" is printed. The original reads: "Je me sens un homme nouveau, un homme fort, puissant, différend de ceux qui se traînent aux pieds de ces géants, géants pour eux parce que vus d'en bas."

[14] Abrons and Essoumas are two groups of peoples from the Ivory Coast. Each of these two groups is a part of the larger Akan people.

[15] The conversations between the narrator and the customs officer (see following page also) lose their impact in translation; I have purposely left them in the original French. The first example shows that the main communication problem between the two is based upon a misunderstanding of practices, while the second example serves to illustrate the problem of pronunciation:

"Pineapples, I say.

Pineapples - se

Pineapples

Pineapples - se."

[16] The sentence is somewhat obscure in the French and has been translated freely. In the original version it reads: "Mode sans doute, mais de sens profond... Son splendide isolement lui pèse désormais le niveau de l'équerre, son mode de raisonnement: 'Comment? pourquoi? donc!' ne se sont pas révélés comme des éléments pouvant donner à l'homme une appréciation exacte de l'existence..." Dadié's point can be understood only within the context of the traditional debate between the West and Africa in which the former represents abstract, analytical and technical knowledge and the latter spontaneous participation in the natural world. The Parisian's need to surround themselves with plants and animals is thus taken as an indication that analyses and technology have been shown to be bankrupt even in the Western world.

[17] This is the one occasion where the four symbols which serve as primary themes in the book are brought together. Cinzano symbolizes advertising and business, butterflies symbolize spontaneity and beauty, the ruins represent the point of contact with the past, and the Bank of the Holy Spirit represents the union of money, religion and Western-style individualism.

[18] In African fiction the commercial district, which is representative of technological pragmatism, exploitation and European capitalism, is often situated on the city's highest ground. Examples of such towns are Tanga in Mongo Beti's Ville Cruelle and Douma in Ferdinand Oyono's Le Vieux Nègre et la Médaille.

[19] There is an obvious misprint in this sentence where "globle" for "globe" appears. The original reads: "Grimpe sur le globle, il parait attendre les hommages du soleil levant."

[20] Fluctuat nec mergitui is the motto of the city of Paris: "Il flotte et il ne sombre pas". Like a ship it floats, but unlike a ship it can never sink.

[21] Qui langue a, à Rome va: He that has a tongue in his head may go where he will.*

*Closets D'Errey, Henride, Proverbes et Idiotismes Français-Anglais. Pondichery, 1939.

[22] marché pour des prunes: worked for nothing

[23] Alea jacta est: The die is cast. Caesar's famous statement as he crossed the Rubicon.

[24] Here Dadié begins with the idiomatic expression "marcher au pas" and in the end gives it a literal translation: "Peut-on réfléchir quand on est pied?" Such literal interpretation of traditional idiomatic expressions is a favorite technique with Dadié

and corresponds, in the realm of language, to his treatment of visual images (See Note 7). In the one case, the extension and development of the author's vision is triggered by a particular image, in the other by the literal meaning of a specific word within the idiomatic expression. This transformation is not apparent in the English translation.

[25]"...qui persuade vous hisser sur le pavois" is incorrect gramatically and is obviously a misprint. The phrase should undoubtedly read: "...qui prétend vous hisser sur le pavois": who proposes to extol you.

[26] American *nigth* (sic) club for American night club.

[27] Slow and steady wins the race.

[28] Quos vult perdere Jupiter dementat: Latin version of Euripedes thought—those whom Jupiter wishes to destroy, he begins by driving mad.

[29] There is an obvious typographical error in the French text which reads: "Aussi le convient—ils dans les restaurants... ." Corrected it should read: "Aussi le conviennent-ils dans les restaurants... ."

[30] le farfalle: butterfly.

[31] Time to eat.

[32] Good evening.

[33] There is a misprint in the French text where "ils" for "il" is printed: "Habituè à prendre des positions, ils me regardait en souriant, savourant sa victoire."

[34] Qui non si muore mai: Here no one dies.

[35] Lambrusco: kind of Italian wine.

[36] Grignolino: type of Piedmontese wine.